FOCUS ON THE FAMILY® LiFE on the™ EdGe

MiND oVer meDia

..The Power of Making Sound..
.......Entertainment Choices

Stan Campbell • Randy Southern

TYNDALE

MIND OVER MEDIA

Copyright © 2001 by Focus on the Family
All rights reserved. International copyright secured.

Library of Congress Cataloging-in-Publication Data

Campbell, Stan.
  Mind over media : the power of making sound entertainment choices /
Stan Campbell, Randy Southern.
      p. cm.
  ISBN 1-56179-870-3
1. Christian teenagers—Religious life. 2. Mass media—Religious
aspects—Christianity. [1. Mass media. 2. Christian life.] I. Southern,
Randy. II. Title.
  BV4531.3 .C36 2001
  241'.65—dc21   00-012430

A Focus on the Family book published by Tyndale House Publishers,
Wheaton, Illinois.

Editor: John Duckworth
Cover design: Lance Blanchard, The Raymond Group
Cartoons: John Duckworth

Printed in the United States of America

01 02 03 04 05 06 07/10 9 8 7 6 5 4 3 2 1

mind over media

..The Power of Making Sound..
........Entertainment Choices

table of contents

Introduction

editor's note:

Before each chapter in this book, you'll see quotes about the media. Unless otherwise noted, these are from young people across America. You may agree with some; others may make you mad. Either way, we hope they give you something to think about.

introduction

Wow! This is a sight we don't see too much these days. There you are, a regular teenager, sitting with a *book* in your hand. Be sure to place yourself on the endangered species list as we take a moment to compose ourselves and keep from weeping openly.

Of course, we assume you're reading this while listening to music, planning what movie to see next, and waiting for something to download on your computer. (That's what *we're* doing as we're writing it.)

Let us introduce ourselves. We're Randy and Stan, and we'll be your authors for this book. We're going to be talking about the media, an area near and dear to our hearts. Both of us have been to school to learn all about the subject, but don't worry. You won't see a lot of communication theory or pie charts in this book.

While we're at it, here are some other things you won't see:

- Scare tactics to stop you from watching and/or listening to your favorite media personalities. ("Didja hear that some girl touched [insert name of 'bad' musician]'s foot at a recent concert, and the next morning she'd started growing horns and a tail?")
- Lots of references to "current" bands and shows that will be outdated by the time you finish reading this introduction.
- Pictures of the authors with sweaters wrapped around their necks, with chin in hand, or in other phony poses.
- Requests for contributions to our nonprofit organization, "The Randy and Stan First Annual Caribbean Media/ Tanning Conference."

What you *should* expect is a mildly humorous book that treats you like a reasonably intelligent reader—and helps you to think about the media choices you make every day.

It's our goal in this book to be absolutely honest with you. We aren't holier-than-thou. We continue to struggle with some of the problem areas, as you do. We also know how confusing, scary, terrible, and wonderful the media can be. After all, we've been watching and listening a little longer than you have (in Stan's case, a *lot* longer).

The first three chapters will cover a lot of basics, so we suggest you read those first. From there on, each chapter deals with a specific topic; you can jump around to the media that most interest you. We've tried very hard, though, to say something important in *every* chapter.

You may not agree with everything we say. That's okay. We don't agree with everything *we* read in Christian media books, either. We simply ask that you consider what we're saying before you reach any final conclusions.

Maybe you saw this book on your bookstore shelf and picked it up. More likely, someone has thrust it upon you. Whatever the reason, we're glad you're holding it. We'll try to keep you turning the pages—at least until the DVD comes out.

◆ ◆ ◆ ◆ ◆ ◆ ◆ ◆ ◆ ◆ ◆ ◆ ◆ ◆ ◆ ◆ ◆ ◆ ◆ ◆ ◆ ◆ ◆ ◆

"Media has a huge impact on society."
—MICHAEL L.

"It hasn't got an effect on me, really."
—MELISSA W.

"The media . . . the right kinds of it . . . have played just as
much [of] a role in promoting the good things as they
have the bad things. There's a lot of good stuff out there."
—TYLER D.

"I just pretty much watch it and take my own opinion of
things. . . . When I was younger . . . media probably did
have a big influence. But, no, not anymore."
—BILL F.

"There's a lot of bad messages through music and on TV
all the time—sex and violence and drugs. And they're not
doing a good enough job to keep that away from us."
—ANDREW G.

"I don't think that the music or the media or
nothing like that affects how I feel."
—DANIEL O.

"What I believe is what I believe. I mean, I don't let anybody influence me. I influence myself."
—RAYMOND R.

"I see all that's going on in the media and I say,
'Lord, keep me from that.'"
—ADRIAN M.

"All types of media really did have a large impact on me."
—LUCAS SALMON, CONVICTED OF RAPE AND MURDER

"I think the media has like a way strong effect.... It's one
of the strongest things that affects teenagers today
because of everything ... from MTV to all the other stations that pretty much ... control a teenager's day."
—NIKE C.

"[Entertainment] influences my life and
a lot of people around me, too."
—ANDREW G.

"People argue, 'Do we affect the media, or does the
media affect us?' I think it's a two-way street. But the
media does affect us, in some way or another."
—KIRK G.

◆ ◆ ◆ ◆ ◆ ◆ ◆ ◆ ◆ ◆ ◆ ◆ ◆ ◆ ◆ ◆ ◆ ◆

"Can you tell me where the 'Revolting but Cheap' section is?"

welcome to the jungle

The Scene:
An emergency meeting of the
Neanderthal Parent-Teacher Association.

Principal Og: If everyone will pull their rocks into a circle, we will begin. I would like to start by thanking Mrs. Gork for alerting us all to a problem. In case you haven't heard, yesterday Ooka was down by the saber-tooth tiger cave telling a story of our ancestors. But when he got to the part about how we defeated our enemies and took their women, his grunts had a disturbingly suggestive tone to them!

Mrs. Gork: I don't know about the rest of you, but I don't want my teenagers exposed to that kind of filth. There's no place for it in a decent society!

Mr. Zook: She's right! Something has to be done about our singers and storytellers. They're having a dangerous effect on our children. Yesterday when I returned from the hunt, I discovered my teenage daughters had pierced parts of their bodies that have no business being pierced. They'd been listening to some Cro-Magnon singing a song called "Pierce It if You Love Me"!

Mr. Oop: I was on the same hunt, and when I got home, my teenagers had painted all over the walls of my cave! I tried to scrub off the drawings, but I think they may be there for good.

Principal Og: It seems clear that today's music and stories are having damaging effects on our young people. You may recall that within a week after fire was discovered, our teenagers were sending inappropriate smoke signals to each other! We must prevent something like that from happening again.

Mr. Zook: Here's an idea. When a singer's music is offensive, we could spread some tree sap on a large leaf and stick it over the person's mouth—to show some sort of parental guidance.

Mr. Gork: Or when Ooka's stories get too sexual or violent, someone standing nearby could poke him with a sharpened, V-shaped flint chip.

Mr. Oop: A V-chip? Hmmm . . .

◆ ◆ ◆

We'll leave the discussion at this point, since this meeting lasted well into the Iron Age.

In fact, the media debate continues today. Maybe you've noticed.

School boards argue over whether to ban certain books from the classroom. Theater owners try (or at least pretend to try) to keep you out of R-rated movies if you're under 17. Advice columnists warn you about stalkers who prowl Web chat rooms, looking for victims. Retailers slap Parental Advisory stickers on CDs. Libraries install filters to keep you from viewing pornography on their computers. Politicians make speeches about preventing you from getting your hands on blood-and-guts video games. Organizations boycott magazine ads that use sex to get you to buy a certain brand of clothes. TV manufacturers offer V-chips to prevent you from watching violent TV shows.

And we haven't even mentioned your parents yet.

It's a jungle out there. At least that's what a lot of people want you to believe about the media. They warn that any innocent, wide-eyed teenager can wander into this media jungle and become lost in the darkness, swallowed by electronic quicksand, or emotionally scarred for life.

Other people say that's a lot of hooey. They claim the media offer no threat to teenagers or anyone else. They say entertainment doesn't create problems, but simply mirrors problems that already exist. The media, these people say, are usually a positive influence.

the downside

Not too many years ago, your world may have been safe and secure. Maybe the primary media influences in your life were Barney, Raffi, VeggieTales, and assorted cartoon shows. But one day you realized you'd reached the end of Sesame Street— and were standing on the edge of a strange, new neighborhood that didn't look anything like Mr. Rogers'. And you didn't have a single Blue's Clue to help you know which way to turn.

Perhaps you were visiting a friend who had access to an older brother's magazines and videos. Maybe you bought a new CD because of a sweet little song you liked, but discovered other lyrics on it that would make Marines blush. Maybe you were exploring the radio dial and found a morning talk show that opened your ears to a whole new vocabulary.

However it started, your transition from child to adult may have been hurried along by the media—faster than you (or your parents) would have preferred. When parents see such changes take place in their "babies," they tend to get alarmed. (Who can blame them, since you're so special?) As a result, sometimes they—and others—are quick to point out the potential downside of entertainment:

- There's too much sex, violence, and profanity in the media. It desensitizes you to bad stuff.
- Teenagers imitate whatever they see and hear, and will probably end up hurting themselves.
- The media shoot for the lowest common denominator among viewers and listeners. Just look at wrestling, trashy talk shows, and gangsta rap lyrics.
- The media present an unrealistic portrayal of life. Sitcoms solve any problem in a half hour; movies are an escape from reality.
- The media waste time and cause us to focus on unimportant things. It's much easier to watch TV reruns than to do algebra homework.
- Most entertainment leaves God out of the picture, giving us an incomplete perspective on how life should be.

the upside

Those are some possible negatives of entertainment. But let's be fair. What about the benefits?

- The media bring people together. From jungle drums to smoke signals to newspapers to radio to television to the

Internet, the media have always assured us that others are around to share our information and emotions.

- The media help you control your environment. When you're driving, working out, or trying to relax, the right song goes a long way in setting the mood. When you're sick, television keeps your attention off your queasy stomach.

- The media help you express yourself. Love, thankfulness, confusion, rage, concern over injustice—at times it's hard to express those feelings. Yet a song, poem, or piece of film dialogue can make you stop what you're doing and think, *That's what I've been trying to say!*

- The media can tear down the walls that separate us from other people. Until they saw on TV in the 1960s the mistreatment of black people, many white viewers were apathetic about the struggle for civil rights. It's one thing to hear about wars in Eastern Europe or Africa, but it's harder to ignore them when we see images of starving or wounded kids.

- The media put you "in the loop." If you've ever experienced "media connectedness," you know what we're talking about. It's that satisfying moment when you hear someone describe a movie or song or website— and you can say, "I saw that movie," or "I just bought that CD," or "I've got that website bookmarked."

your side

What do *you* think? Here are a few questions to consider. All we ask is that you're honest, whatever your opinions— because we promise to be the same in this book.

1. What statement best describes your feelings toward the media?

___ My media experiences are mostly positive, but occasionally the bad stuff scares me.

___ Most media options are dangerous, unless they're put out by Christians.

___ There's some bad stuff out there, but I try to look for the good.

___ I'm not sure what's out there, but I'm getting curious.

___ I'll watch or listen to anything—it won't affect me.

___ Other

2. How do your parents feel about your media involvement?

___ They always want to tell me what I can and can't watch/read/listen to.

___ They offer strong opinions, but leave the final choices up to me.

___ They stay out of my life and let me make my own decisions.

___ Their own media choices are a lot worse than mine.

___ Other

3. When you encounter a media hazard—something you see or hear that you suspect might not be good for you—what do you do?

___ Secretly enjoy it and hope nobody else notices.

___ Keep watching or listening, but feel guilty.

___ Turn my attention elsewhere as quickly as possible.

___ Protest with letters and boycotts.

___ Warn others to avoid those things.

___ Throw a party and tell all my wicked friends what I've found.

___ Other

4. Which media hazards seem to have the strongest effects on you? Choose all that apply.

___ Sexual images or lyrics

___ Violent images or lyrics

___ Profanity

___ Ads and commercials that make me feel inferior

___ Internet relationships that have an element of mystery or even danger

___ Other

5. How do your friends and peers seem to be affected by their entertainment choices?

___ I don't know anyone who has serious problems.

___ Maybe a few people I know are a little too absorbed in certain media.

___ I know some people who are really starting to get messed up.

___ It's awful! I'm surrounded by media junkies!

___ Other

6. Suppose you had to give up each of the following things for a year. At the end of that year, would you be better off (B), about the same (S), worse (W), or totally insane (I)?

___ Books

___ Magazines

___ Music

___ The Internet

___ Television

___ Movies/Videos

___ Computer/Video Games

___ Advertisements

7. Finally, which of the following best reflects your feelings as you begin this book?

___ I already know what you're going to tell me. I predict it'll be a waste of my time.

___ You haven't slammed any of my favorites yet, so I'll keep reading until you do.

___ I think I have an open mind. I'll consider what you have to say.

___ Frankly, I could use a little insight about how the media might affect me.

___ Other

our side

If we were you, we'd probably be wondering about the guys who are writing this book. Who do we think we are? Do we even *watch* TV? Do we know the difference between a CD and a DVD? When was the last time we listened to anything but the oldies station on the radio? How much do we even *know* about today's media?

Let's look first at Stan. He was a month shy of 14 when the original Woodstock took place, but didn't get to go because he had to stay home and mow the yard. Still, he went on to get a degree in recording industry management and another graduate degree in communications. He watched plenty of TV and listened to a lot of music when he was a teenager—and still does. He's been a church youth director for about 20 years and has tried to keep up with his students' changing media tastes during that whole time.

Then there's Randy. He's incapable of changing a light bulb without illustrated instructions, but he can name every album

Elvis Costello ever recorded, recite Monty Python skits from memory, and talk for an hour about why certain movies should be considered American comedy classics. In high school he decided his future lay in music videos; when the market for video directors dried up, he took a job as a book editor and later became a freelance writer. He's written about the media before, but not nearly as interestingly or as intelligently as in this book.

Both of us—Stan and Randy—are the kind of guys who eagerly anticipate new books, movies, CD releases, and more. We try to be creative in our writing and relationships, and the media is loaded with lessons in creative expression—some of which we choose to ignore, but others which cause us to stand in awe.

Certain songs say more in three verses and a chorus than we could stuff into a hundred pages. Some movie scenes express emotions that help us better relate to our wives, kids, parents, and friends. Some artists—and not necessarily Christian ones—ask tough questions about God that challenge us spiritually.

But we've also learned to deal with the media in much the same way that we choose friends. Like us, you probably have only a few friends who have proven to be trustworthy. At the other end of the spectrum are a few people you may want to avoid at all costs. Between these two extremes are a horde of other people with whom you interact at various levels—some closely, some cautiously.

In the same way, a few media sources will become best friends to you. Others should be avoided altogether. In between are millions of other possible sources that may or may not turn out to be your friends.

your mind, your media

As far as we're concerned, here's the basic question this book tries to answer: *How can we learn to control how much the media influence us?*

People argue about exactly how bad that influence gets. But if the media have *any* kind of influence—good *or* bad— don't you want to be aware of it?

After all, it's your brain—your life.

Consider the following true story.

In 1988 a Dallas morning deejay asked his listeners to send him $20. He didn't explain why. Even though Dallas was in the middle of an economic recession, within a week the radio station had received more than $240,000.

That's right. More than 12,000 people sent in their hard-earned money just because a radio personality asked them to. The money was donated to charities, so no harm was done. But the point is that *it's usually a good idea to ask some questions before automatically responding to the media.* Next time, the results might not be so positive.

If you're honest in thinking through these things, you can make entertainment choices that enrich your life. If you stay aware of what's going on around you, your relationship with the media can be as enjoyable as a walk in the woods.

But if you don't, it can be a jungle out there.

◆ ◆

"You have a right to listen to what you want to. . . . No matter what, it will affect you, but . . . you can listen to it and not do it. There's a lot of people that listen to [a controversial band] that are . . . perfectly fine people and they're doing nothing wrong, because they chose not to. . . . It's a personal choice that you have to make."
—*NIKE C.*

"I think that the media can interpret relationships and have an influence on [teenagers] as far as becoming sexually active. Because people look at the movies and stuff and they'll think, 'Oh, well, they're having sex. This is what it's like to be in love.' And then they'll do the same."
—*ELIZABETH S.*

"If you watch a guy on TV doing drugs or something, he's got all the . . . girls at the club or whatever. You want to be like that person. . . . A lot of kids watch wrestling and get all hyped up and want to go and wrestle outside or some crazy things like that. . . . Everything has big influences."
—*BILL F.*

"To do that to somebody with a gun or kick someone in the face or . . . punch 'em . . . you'd see that on the movies and TV. That's where you get it."
—*BILLY H.*

"A lot of people who claim that media is a big influence on . . . crime, I think it's just like a big cop-out."
—*RAY P.*

"I just watch what is fun for me. . . . There's no limits."
—*RICK L.*

"If I see . . . a violent movie, it's not going to affect me. . . . I'm [not] going to go and copy what they did 'cause I know that's wrong. So it doesn't really affect me unless it's in a good way."
—*ERIKA T.*

"You can make all the movies you want and write anything you want and people are going to watch it. . . . It's on them what they do afterwards."
—*AARON B.*

"What someone likes to spend their free time doing tells a lot about them. Say, if a guy is watching wrestling every day . . . he's not gonna be the number-one pick for me."
—*SHOLÉ G.*

"Certain things that the media portrays allow us to think, 'Maybe, well, that's okay,' or, 'Maybe this is normal.' . . . Even though we know it's not right, we start to rationalize and let ourselves believe that it is."
—*JONATHAN H.*

"A lot of kids try to deny that . . . watching a bad movie or listening to a [certain] CD won't affect them in a negative way, but I think it really does. I used to think that same way . . . before I got into prison."
—*LUCAS SALMON, CONVICTED OF RAPE AND MURDER*

"We all feel, 'It's not affecting me. It's affecting them, not me.' But I feel . . . if you pray and really ask God to show you, I think . . . He'll let you know . . . if what you're watching or what you're intaking is really not of Him and if you should leave it alone."
—*CHARLES H.*

◆ ◆ ◆ ◆ ◆ ◆ ◆ ◆ ◆ ◆ ◆ ◆ ◆ ◆ ◆ ◆ ◆ ◆ ◆ ◆

"Son, your mother and I are concerned about the effect
your media choices may be having on you."

no big deal?

I'm a 15-year-old girl who reads *Brio* magazine, and I have read reviews in the [*Chart Watch*] book. I, for the most part, respect your opinions on music. However, I was looking up the soundtrack to my favorite movie . . . today, and it linked to your review of it. . . . Why do adults always assume things teens do are because of their music? You're making it sound like this music will drive people to kill others. This is totally wrong. . . . I'm a fairly solid Christian, and still listen to some of this kind of music, and I just like the sound. It doesn't influence me in bad ways. I am not a murderer. I don't smoke, drink, or do drugs.

—Beth*

---

* "Beth" is not the author's real name. We gave her an alias to protect her identity. Just to be safe, we also changed the names of "Beth's" parents and siblings and moved the entire family to a heavily guarded compound in an unnamed South American country.

Obviously not everyone believes the media are something to worry about. Many people, like Beth, feel that restricting the things we see and hear—or blaming those things for the evil in our world—is overreacting.

People like Beth often give three reasons for their view:

1. "It's just entertainment."

2. "The things we see and hear in the media don't affect the way we act."

3. "The media simply reflect what's going on in society."

Let's take a closer look at those reasons. Decide for yourself whether they hold up.

reason #1: "it's just entertainment."

You're making a big deal out of nothing. The world is compli-cated, confusing, and stressful; television, the Internet, movies, and video games help us escape the pressures of everyday life. With all the really serious problems in the world today, it doesn't make sense to get your underwear in a bunch about things that aren't even real.

If you're nodding your head in agreement, join the crowd. Sometimes it seems media opponents go too far in looking for things to object to. Let's put it this way: If you're pausing your VCR during *Pinocchio* to make sure all the puppets on Geppetto's workbench are fully clothed, maybe the media aren't your most pressing problem.

It's easy (and tempting) to make fun of people who go overboard in knocking the media. But isn't it just as goofy to say that everything we watch, play, listen to, and read is unimportant?

After all, saying "just entertainment" is like saying "just school" or "just food" or "just money." These are all things that matter to us; they play big roles in our everyday lives. That's why we (usually) try to make smart decisions about what to study, eat, and buy.

We may feel like putting entertainment into a separate category because it doesn't seem "real." But there's no reason to believe it's any less important than other areas of our lives— especially when so many of us spend so much time and cash being entertained.

There's another reason why our entertainment choices may be more important than we think. It's this: The fact that we find certain things *entertaining* says a lot about us.

At any given moment in your life, you have hundreds—if not thousands—of entertainment options. Why do you choose the ones you do? Why do you react positively to some things and negatively to others?

- Why do some songs make you reach for the volume dial and others make you reach for the tuning dial?
- Why do you love some TV shows and despise others?
- Why do some movies leave you breathless and others leave you nauseated?
- Why are some video games addictive to you while others seem lame?

No, you can't judge a person based on one or two media choices. But you can get a clue. All your entertainment choices are small pieces in the puzzle of you.

Think for a minute about your favorite movies, TV shows, performers, bands, songs, video games, websites, magazines, and books. Better yet, write them on a sheet of paper. See any common themes? What might people say about you if they saw your list? Would they be right?

Ben wrote down some of his favorites, even though the

idea of making a list seemed too much like homework. Here's what he came up with:

Favorite movie: The *Scream* movies

Favorite TV show: *Celebrity Deathmatch*

Favorite music: Any hardcore rap or metal

Favorite computer game: *Duke Nukem*

Favorite book: Anything by Stephen King

Mike, one of Ben's friends, found the list. "I've got two words for you, dude," Mike said after reading it. "Anger management."

Ben looked at his list again and had to laugh. He'd never thought of himself as a violent person, yet most of the things he'd written down involved people beating or killing each other. He tried to come up with a snappy comeback for Mike, but couldn't.

"Just" entertainment? Or is it a part of your life, like all the other parts—one that says a lot about what's going on inside of you?

reason #2: "the things we see and hear in the media don't affect the way we act."

People are always trying to blame the media for things crimi-nals and wackos do. The media can't make people do things they wouldn't do otherwise.

If you don't believe the media affect the way we act, well, *excuuuse me!*

(Ancient history note: In case you're wondering, "Excuuuse me" was an expression comedian Steve Martin coined over a quarter century ago. He started saying it in his standup act, made it popular on one of his comedy albums, and then turned it into a national catchphrase when he used it on *Saturday Night*

Live. Before long, it seemed like everyone was saying it. Some people, most of them pretty old, still use the phrase today.)

Think of some of your own favorite expressions. Don't a lot of them come from movies, TV shows, commercials, or songs? *Yeah, baby.*

Is there anything wrong with parroting expressions we hear in the media? Maybe not, depending on the expression. But the whole idea of catchphrases shows that the media can affect us, sometimes in ways we don't even recognize.

If the process were a movie, it might be called *Attack of the Brain Hijackers.*

Here's how it works. Have you ever turned on a really stupid movie or ultra-lame TV show—then sat there and watched it all the way through? All the while you're telling yourself, "I can't believe how dumb this is." Yet you keep watching. Most of us have done it. Why?

Because certain media have direct access to the control panel of our brains. They climb into our cerebral cortex, rev our Sensory Enjoyment tachometer up to 11, and shift our Rational Thought into low gear. With someone else behind the wheel of our brains, that makes us *passengers.* Things that we might ordinarily object to—or at least question—pass unnoticed because we're too busy enjoying the ride.

Consider these examples:

James is sitting in front of the tube on a Saturday night, watching his favorite martial-arts cop show. For 50 minutes he's watched the bad guys firebomb an orphanage, hijack a school bus, and beat up a dozen or so nuns. Now, with 10 minutes left in the show, it's time for the hero's revenge.

James is ready for it. He knows there's only one way to deal with villains like these—through bone-crunching punches to the face and roundhouse kicks to the side of the head, preferably in slow motion. James, who normally would agree with ideas like "Love your enemies" (Luke 6:27), watches with satisfaction as the evildoers get the tar beaten out of them by the star of the show.

Gillian is watching a movie with her friends. It's a romantic comedy about a guy and girl in high school who start out hating each other, but gradually fall in love. He's a troublemaking football player with a reputation for using girls; she's an uptight, straight-A student who doesn't believe in sex before marriage.

Finally, at the prom, the guy announces to everyone that he's willing to wait as long as it takes to be with his true love. The girl is so moved that she tells the crowd she's ready to "prove" her love physically. Everybody at the prom whoops and cheers; a romantic ballad plays on the soundtrack as the two lovebirds go to the guy's house and prepare for a night of passion.

Gillian smiles from ear to ear. She loves happy endings. Even though she would say she's against premarital sex, the idea of the couple in the movie "proving" their love *feels* like a happy ending.

Will James, having watched a violent TV show, beat up the next person who makes fun of him? Will Gillian wind up an unwed mother because she cheered at the end of that romantic comedy?

Probably not. But for a short time, both of them handed the keys to their brains over to the media and climbed into the back seat to go along for the ride. For about an hour, James accepted the philosophy that violence is the best way to deal with enemies. After 90 minutes, Gillian was ready to believe that sex before marriage can be a good thing.

Giving up control of your brain for 30 minutes here and 90 minutes there may not seem like a big deal. We all need to "veg out" now and then, right? But add up all the TV and movies you watch, music you listen to, books and magazines you read, video games you play . . . and you'll see how much mileage the media may be putting on your gray matter.

reason #3: "the media simply reflect what's going on in society."

The media aren't the problem—society is. The media simply hold a mirror up to the world around us. There's violence in computer games because we live in a violent society. There's sex on TV because sex is a major issue in most people's lives. Instead of blaming the media, we should be grateful to them for making us more aware of the world we live in.

This is a brilliant argument for two reasons. First, it makes entertainment producers the heroes. If not for them, we'd be clueless about what the world is really like, right? Take that argument a little further, and it looks like the more deeply involved in the media you become, the more you'll learn about the world.

Second, this argument gives people in the media free rein to do pretty much whatever they want. No matter how perverted a movie is or how revolting a song is, it can be defended with one simple phrase: "Don't blame us—we're just the messengers!"

Is it fair to blame the media for problems in society, or should we blame society for problems in the media?

Maybe we should call it a draw and blame both sides. The

media do reflect things that go on in society, and can help us understand the world. But the *way* the media portray life can create a whole new set of problems.

Take, for example, the topic of urban life. One way of portraying it is to make a movie about two young men trying to use their basketball skills to escape poverty in inner city Chicago. The film could help audiences understand the tragic stories that are played out every day in urban America.

Another way would be to produce an album of hardcore rap that brags about rape, killing, and gangs. By glorifying the worst aspects of inner city life, the artists may actually be *enticing* young people into the same dead-end life they describe.

Wouldn't it be hypocritical to give the media credit for the movie without holding them responsible for the songs?

As for entertainment holding a mirror up to society, we have one question: Where are all the ugly people in the media—or even the plain-looking people? To put it another way, how many movie idols, TV performers, or rock stars look like the people you hang out with? Unless you're good buddies with a bunch of supermodels, the answer is probably not many.

More often than not, the media "mirror" a world where everyone is hardbodied (or at least funny). Where does that leave the rest of us—the ones who didn't hit the jackpot in the genetic lottery?

Sure, the media portray a world. Sometimes it's the real one. Sometimes, though, it's a fantasy.

how big a deal?

So, is Beth right? Are some media watchdogs a little too rabid?

Are some media defenders a little dishonest?

Are both true?

We'll let you decide.

In the meantime, you might think about buying a used car.

Here's what we mean. Maybe it's a good idea to treat entertainment producers as if they were used car dealers trying to sell you an automobile. You may not be able to trust everything you see and hear.

But if you keep your brain working and your attitude skeptical, you may just come away with something you can use.

◆ ◆

"When I was younger, my parents tried to stop me from watching certain things. But it was easy back then to go find it, and I think it's even easier now."
—*DARREN F.*

"I do [care what my parents think about my media choices]. I respect my parents and . . . how they live. . . . They've provided for me a lot in my life, so I think I should at least give them some respect."
—*NEIL G.*

"I think I will probably in the future change and set more limits for myself. Right now I haven't really. . . . I don't know if it's . . . a stage I'm at right now, if I haven't . . . just matured enough. . . . When you have that freedom you just wanna go out and watch whatever. . . . Once you turn 17 and you can get into R-rated movies, then it's like, 'Yeah, I can get in. I'll just go in and watch it anyway.'"
—*KHRISTEN B.*

"I don't want the things that I see or hear . . . if I see them too much, for them to start to seep in and I start to think that's a normal way of life or that's the right thing to do."
—*JENNIFER B.*

"Yes, I have placed personal limits on what I watch and what I listen to. I try not to listen to anything that has vulgar language, or that has sexual content, or that has extreme violence."
—*TIFFANY J.*

"Guarding my heart would look like me not allowing anything to come in that would cause my heart to kind of slip away from God or to . . . trust anything but Him."
—*JENNIFER B.*

"Who determines what normal is? We need to determine it by the Word of God. We need to know what our Creator [thinks]. The One who made us knows what's best. Not MTV, you know—not the media of today. We need to pick up our Bibles and find out for ourselves how we're meant to be living."
—*PHIL JOEL, BASS PLAYER, THE NEWSBOYS*

"It really bothers me when I see certain things that are socially accepted in society and then I read [the Bible] and I see that this is not what God has for me. This is not what He wants me to watch. And certain things that I know the Bible says I'm not supposed to do, I try not to watch those things [or] listen to those things."
—*TIFFANY J.*

"[God] sent His Son down to die for you, and . . . you should just take that into consideration. When you see what He's done for you, why fill your heart and your mind with things like that that will hurt Him? . . . To me it just doesn't make sense."
—*MARLYNE J.*

"This world's gonna waste away. The media's gonna go with it. All that's really gonna count is your relationship with God."
—*CHRISTY C.*

◆ ◆

"Mom, PG-13 does *not* mean 13 parents are supposed to watch the movie with you!"

your turn to discern

What's an average morning like for you? Let us guess.

First, you scream at the top of your lungs so Mom will come into your room, powder your cute little behind, and give you a fresh diaper. Ah, that smells better! Then she puts on your yellow bunny bib for a big breakfast of milk (you're on the bottle now!), strained carrots, and smushed pears for dessert. Then, as an extra-special treat, she scatters Cheerios across your high chair tray and you spend glorious hours sticking them in your nose and ears.

No?

Okay, maybe you're past this stage of life. But at one time this was probably how you spent your days. By now you're probably able to powder your own behind and change your own diapers. And you've moved on to solid foods.

You're probably able to do a few other things, too—like making your own media choices.

Kristin, a junior in high school, hasn't had much practice in this area. Her parents decided years ago that the family would avoid all TV and movies, and to allow Kristin to listen only to Christian music. It wasn't so terrible when she was younger. But now she feels she's missing out on a lot—not all of it bad. It's hard for her to meet new people because the conversation always turns to favorite bands and shows. She doesn't like this growing feeling of isolation—and is secretly eager to go away to college and "do a lot of catching up."

Will Kristin be ready to make good media choices? Now that she—and you—are on the edge of adulthood, we'd like to help the two of you make some decisions for yourself.

After all, you're not a little kid anymore.

if it's not one wing, it's a rudder

Think of your life in terms of an airplane disaster movie.

Suppose the pilots (your parents, teachers, other authorities) have all eaten bad airline food and are hurling in the aisle, completely helpless. The plane of your life is threatening to veer off course and go down in flames if somebody doesn't do something. It's up to you to step into the cockpit, sit down at the controls, and fly this baby!

But don't worry. We're going to talk you through it.

As you take the wheel and look out at the potential media hazards that threaten to bring you down, the first button you need to push is labeled *Discernment.*

All discernment means is consciously deciding what you will and won't allow to take root in your mind. Discernment is determining what's all right for you to get involved with and filtering out the potentially harmful stuff in the media jungle.

Perhaps other people have been doing this for you so far. But you're going to need to take over if you want to venture safely from here.

the "why" files

Before we go any further, let's deal with those big questions on your mind. Go ahead, ask them! Get them out in the open!

"All right," you say. "Why bother with discernment? Why go to all the trouble of identifying messages and evaluating how they affect me? Why can't I just sit back and enjoy the media like I would a roller coaster?"

Good questions! Discernment *is* work at times. And when it comes to entertainment, who wants to fool with work?

It might be nice if the media were like other forms of entertainment, such as roller coasters, baseball, or knitting pet sweaters. But with the media, you're continually receiving and processing lyrics, images, imaginative possibilities, philosophies, messages. In other words, your *mind* gets involved.

Jesus had something to say about our minds. The whole point of all the commands in the Bible, He said, could be summed up this way: "Love the Lord your God with all your heart and with all your soul and with all your mind" (Matthew 22:37).

"Wait a minute," you might say. "Why are you quoting Bible verses at me? I thought this book was about entertainment, not church."

Another good question. Why should you care what Jesus has to say about your mind—or anything else, for that matter?

If you don't claim to be a follower of Jesus, we guess you wouldn't have any reason to care yet. But if you do make that claim, you're saying two important things about yourself:

1. You have a relationship with God through His Son, Jesus.

2. You don't want anything to get in the way of that relationship.

If those things aren't true of you, we hope you'll talk to a

Christian friend or youth pastor about how to start that kind of relationship. If you *are* a Christian, we assume you realize that your faith is connected to every part of your life, not just "church."

Parker is a guy who doesn't seem to realize that. When he's at the church youth group, he says all the "right" things. He even *thinks* a lot of the right things, like believing that lying and greed and premarital sex are wrong, and love and praying and sharing one's faith are good. But when he puts on the headphones of his CD player or enters the darkness of a movie theater or goes online, it's a whole other world. Without thinking about it, he shuts the door on "church stuff" and enters a mental Twilight Zone where Jesus and rules don't seem to apply.

The only problem is that Jesus doesn't see it that way. He said "*all* your mind." He didn't say to devote 90 percent of your mind to God and have 10 percent left over for an "entertainment center" in which He's not welcome.

If you're trying to keep your media choices in a sealed-off compartment where God isn't supposed to go, or if you're devoting time, money, thought, passion, and/or love to media that ought to be going to God, maybe you need to consider who has the keys to your brain.

Don't take our word for it. Take God's Word:

- We're to follow in Jesus' footsteps (1 John 2:6). Remember those "WWJD?" bracelets and T-shirts? "What would Jesus do?" is not always an easy question to answer. But it's a good one to ask when you're making entertainment choices. Would He snap up that CD or shut it off? Watch the movie or walk out? Or might He do something else entirely?

- We should keep our mental focus on positive things (Philippians 4:8).
- Certain things (such as using profanity and telling sex jokes) are off limits (Ephesians 5:3-7).
- A real relationship with God should be changing us for the better (Romans 12:1-2).
- Even as teenagers, we should keep respecting parents and others in authority (Luke 2:48-52; Romans 13:1-2).

That last one might be especially tough for Kristin, whose parents barred her from all TV and movies and most music. If she takes the Bible seriously, though, she needs to follow her parents' rules—even if she works to prove to them that she can be trusted with a little more freedom.

and now, back to our feature presentation

Let's return to that airplane disaster movie. You're on your own, trying to land.

Or are you?

Look to your right. Do you have a copilot you didn't count on? Is it someone you can trust? Someone who has the same commitment to Jesus that you do?

If someone else is sharing the controls, he or she might be trying to set a course for a place you don't want to go. *You* need to make the decisions and execute the flight plan.

So as you sit at the control panel of your life, let's start with a checklist of two questions to ask when you're faced with a media choice.

Question #1: What's the message?

Sometimes you can't miss the intended message:

- "Only you can prevent forest fires."
- "Don't drink and drive."

- "Mamas, don't let your babies grow up to be cowboys."

Other messages may not be stated in so many words, yet they come through clearly:

- "Sex may not be right for everyone, but it's a perfectly natural way for some couples who want to show their love to one another."
- "You may not have any gay friends, but homosexuality is the only workable lifestyle for some people."
- "Religious leaders usually seem nice, but they're often hypocritical and offer only shallow answers for life's problems."

Still other messages are "hidden" underneath more obvious ones:

- *Obvious message:* "Blisterine blasts away zits!" *Hidden message:* "A face with zits never gets asked out."

These are common themes of movies, TV shows, songs, and advertising. You might not agree with them. But if you're not pressing that *Discernment* button, and if you hear these messages over and over, you may eventually change your attitude without even thinking about it. That's why evaluating everything you see and hear is a good idea.

Say you're watching a film in which an unmarried girl is caught up in a sexual relationship where she's being manipulated by the guy. Is the message that her friends should care enough to help her get out of the relationship? Or is the message that there's nothing wrong with premarital sex? That's something else entirely.

Or say you're watching a sitcom that pokes fun at a bumbling minister. Is the message that all ministers are that way? As you watch, maybe you need to remind yourself that most pastors are sincere, hard-working, capable people with feelings like yours.

Question #2: What do you think about the presentation of the message?

After you've figured out the message, it's time to evaluate the "package" that message is wrapped in.

A lot of people get this backwards. They start with the package. They fall in love with the wrapping and just accept whatever happens to be inside. For instance, someone might say, "I love country music." But country music can be wrapping paper for all kinds of messages. Some country songs reflect Christian values; others are outright anti-God.

The same is true of rock, rap, movies, TV shows, and most other media options. Saying, "I love action movies!" is like saying, "I love meat!" Some meat is prime beef; other meat is raccoon.

Since so many people don't think past the packaging, you'd better believe media producers put a lot of thought into making it attractive to you. Some of the main ingredients: humor, cartoons, shock value, sex, brutal honesty, scare tactics, and endorsements by your favorite stars.

The formula usually works.

For example, Michael never used to swear. But he finds it so cute when those little cartoon kids on Comedy Central curse like sailors with Tourette's Syndrome. He started out imitating them to be funny, but now he's beginning to swear all the time without even realizing it.

Then there's Bill. He has a mad crush on a particular teenage female recording artist who always appears in short, tight skirts and skimpy tops. He buys every CD she releases the day it comes out. He also "buys" everything she says. If she sings that she loves "men in glasses who cut their classes," you can bet he'll ditch geometry the next day to visit the optometrist. He's so absorbed in the wrapping (the cute singer) that he gives the message little consideration. (And his friends think he's rather pathetic.)

So not every pretty package contains a worthwhile message. On the other hand, sometimes you'll find a good message inside some unusual wrapping.

For example, Ryan likes a band known for its jackhammer percussion and guitar distortions—much too hardcore for many of his friends to appreciate. The group doesn't use profanity, but sings of pain, hatred, and prejudice. A closer look at their lyrics reveals a Christian message about those themes.

The band doesn't choose to be labeled as "Christian rock"; it plays arenas with other bands that are far from Christian. The musicians reach people who would never set foot in a church—the ones who go for the hardcore "packaging" and stumble onto a message they didn't expect.

Once you unwrap the message, you can decide whether or not you like the paper. But if you do it the other way around, you may be buying a box lunch that contains a snake, not a snack.

how low can you go?

"Okay," you might be saying. (How come you keep interrupting? Do you always talk to books?) "Let's cut to the chase. How much sex, violence, and profanity can I see and hear without going too far?"

Nothing personal, but that's the wrong question.

A better one is, "Am I loving God more completely with my heart, mind, and soul in all areas of my life, including my media choices?"

If you're trying to love God more, you're at least headed in the right direction.

If you're asking, "How much crud do I get to see?" you probably aren't.

Take Rudy, for example. He's learned not to go to movies that have nude scenes. Yet any love scene—or newspaper bra ad, for that matter—can prompt him to fantasize about sex. Is his main problem knowing exactly where to draw the line—or is it that his mind isn't fully devoted to God?

Darla's mom is clear about what songs she doesn't want Darla listening to. Those are the first CDs Darla will buy and keep hidden. Does she need to draw the line in a slightly different place—or change her attitude?

Let's face it. Sometimes the media get blamed for a lot of sins that would exist even if music, movies, and the Internet didn't. If we bring lust, rebellion, or selfishness to the media table, we'll have trouble no matter where we draw the line.

In upcoming chapters we'll deal with more specifics about the problem areas. For now we want to paint you the big picture: Your relationship with God is worth a lot. Things that help that relationship grow deeper and stronger are usually worth exploring. Things that mess it up aren't.

Discernment is all about telling the difference.

be an animal—go ahead, be two

Perhaps you've seen the statue of the three monkeys—the first covering its eyes, the second its ears, and the third its mouth. The message is, "See no evil, hear no evil, speak no evil."

Maybe it's not a bad goal for discernment. But should we shield our eyes and ears from all forms of media that mention adultery, child sacrifice, cannibalism, decapitation, seduction, and cold-blooded murder? If we do, the Bible will have to go—because it contains accounts of all these things. Sex, violence, and spiritual struggles are part of Scripture because they're part of life.

So the three monkeys may not be the best model for us. Nor is the ostrich that plunges its head into the sand to avoid reality.

Jesus has a better pair of animals for us to learn from. When He was sending His disciples out to encounter the real world without Him, He told them to "Be as shrewd as snakes and as innocent as doves" (Matthew 10:16). His advice remains an excellent motto for anybody who wants to make wise media choices.

We need to be shrewd enough to see past the wrapping and zero in on the message. As we do that we can be "as innocent as doves" by refusing to fall for messages or packages that get in the way of our relationship with God.

We'll have a lot more to say about discernment in upcoming chapters. For now, start small. Give the following a try this week. Whether you're reading a novel, watching TV or a movie, listening to a new CD, playing a video game, or skimming a magazine article, try your hand at discernment. Ask:

- *What messages, in-my-face or subtle, is the medium trying to communicate?*
- *How do I feel about* how *the message is presented?*
- *If Jesus were faced with this media choice, what might He do?*

The better you get at discernment, the better you'll be able to fly that plane on your own. That's a good thing—because even though a lot of things about you will change throughout your lifetime, your need for discernment never will.

◆ ◆

"The way I dress and the way I talk . . . the music influences me in that way."
—*ANDREW G.*

"I know music's had an immense effect on me growing up. . . . That's how we become the people we become these days. It's not so much our families. Unfortunately, the media has in some ways become our parents."
—*PHIL JOEL, BASS PLAYER, THE NEWSBOYS*

"I know sometimes, like when I'm sad or upset or anything, I find myself just wanting to listen to music—just because it's relaxing. . . . And, in a way, if you're upset over the loss of a boyfriend or a . . . girlfriend, it can just make you dwell on it more. So I think it can impact your mood and make you even more depressed or make you do things you wouldn't normally do."
—*SARAH S.*

"If you listen to a song repeatedly . . . saying that you're nothing but trouble, and if people keep telling you you're nothing but trouble, then you're going to be nothing but trouble."
—*XICA B.*

"Music is an important factor in your life. The lyrics are really going to get into your heart, get into your soul. . . . This may sound strange, but it becomes part of who you are."
—*LUCAS SALMON, CONVICTED OF RAPE AND MURDER*

"I've also changed the radio a lot of times when songs will come on, you know, that are just talking about sex and things that I don't want to hear. So I'll often change the channel."
—*SARAH S.*

"I was in Cleveland and there was a teenager who was really into this band. Their lyrics were real dark, real depressing. . . . He emulated everything they stood for. He became depressed and he fed off one of their songs, which was a pro-suicide song. [He] started givin' his stuff away and . . . wrote out . . . suicide notes [with] the lyrics [from] his favorite group. He then went out to the garage, put in their tape, cranked it up, and he killed himself in the garage. . . . I had a chance to speak to that group a while after that and they basically said they had nothing to do with this."

—PHIL CHALMERS, YOUTH SPEAKER

"I have a friend who was 16 years old. . . . He was with friends that went to rob a furniture store and he was shot 16 times. . . . You know, if this one rapper said he could do it, then [my friend thought he could] do it, too. And he never walked out of that building after he walked in. . . . They're just telling the average body, 'You can do this, you can do that, don't worry about it.' But they're not telling you also that when you walk into [that] store, you're not going to walk out."

—XICA B.

"I don't think that you're going to go out and do crazy things if you listen to this music. It's a possibility. But I want you to examine your heart and your spiritual walk and see if . . . even if it may not kill you physically, is it killing you spiritually? That is my main message. How is it effecting you spiritually? How's your joy? How's your faith? And how is your walk with Christ?"

—PHIL CHALMERS, YOUTH SPEAKER

◆ ◆

"Of *course* I don't listen to the lyrics, man. After two years
with this sound system, I can't even *hear* them."

music: tuned in or tune din?

Psychiatrist: Good morning. What seems to be the problem?

Teenager: Oh, doctor, I'm desperate! I need your help. I hear voices!

Psychiatrist: When do you hear these voices?

Teenager: All the time! Some nights I can hardly get to sleep because of them, and they wake me up in the morning. They're in the car when I'm driving. I hear them in elevators, doctors' offices, and while shopping at the mall. They even follow me when I'm jogging.

Psychiatrist: What do these voices say?

Teenager: Sometimes they tell me they will always love me, and that a change will do me good. Other times they're a little scary.

Psychiatrist: Like when?

Teenager: Some of them say they will rock me—but they don't sound very comforting! And sometimes they ask me weird questions. They want to know who will save my soul. And they ask me what I want, what I really, really want.

Psychiatrist: Do they ever tell you to hurt yourself?

Teenager: Not usually—but they tell me to live *la vida loca,* the crazy life. They also tell me about jagged little pills.

Psychiatrist: Well, I can prescribe a remedy. But many people are unable to complete this drastic course of therapy.

Teenager: What is it, doctor? I'll do anything!

Psychiatrist: You must turn off all your radios, CD players, sleep timers, Walkmans, and all other sources of music. Only then will you find silence and peace from all the voices.

Teenager: *What?* I may be crazy, but I'm not *that* crazy! (*Runs screaming from office.*)

◆ ◆ ◆

We tend to question the mental health of people who hear "little voices" telling them what to do. So why do we voluntarily immerse ourselves in music?

Some of us have radios, tape players, and CD players in our bedrooms, bathrooms, cars, and computers. In between—just in case we're in danger of five minutes of silence, conversation, or the sounds of nature—we have portable players we can strap on and tote with us.

Is the *amount* of music you listen to a problem? How about *what* you're listening to?

my ears are alive with the sound of music

First, let's see how deeply involved you are in music. Look through the following list and check off your answers.

Have you ever used music to:

Wake you up?	___ Yes ___ No
Put you to sleep?	___ Yes ___ No

Pump you up? ___ Yes ___ No
Get you through a tough study period? ___ Yes ___ No
Shock someone (with volume or lyrics)? ___ Yes ___ No
Reinforce your mood (blue, angry, quiet)? ___ Yes ___ No
Change your mood? ___ Yes ___ No
Get romantic? ___ Yes ___ No
Help you express yourself? ___ Yes ___ No
Get a party going? ___ Yes ___ No
Keep you company? ___ Yes ___ No
Fill the silence? ___ Yes ___ No

If you're like most of us, you probably checked several "Yes" answers. Now suppose that we'd asked you the same questions about using drugs or alcohol instead of music. Wouldn't a lot of yes answers indicate an addiction?

Sure, chemical addiction is more life-threatening than listening to a lot of music is. But here's a question: What's the problem with silence? Are you using music simply for enrichment and entertainment, or are you trying to fill a more serious void in your life? Could you be *addicted to* music?

We've known some kids who seem to fit that description. Here's an evaluation sheet one of them filled out after a recent retreat:

Q: What did you like best?

A: The wonderful interaction we had and how we got to feeling so close to each other over the weekend.

Q: What did you like least?

A: You wouldn't let us take our Walkmans.

See any irony here? If all the kids walked around with Walkmans strapped to their heads, how would they ever have the interaction and conversation that meant so much to them?

We can't tell you how many minutes, hours, or days a week you should listen to music. We can only suggest asking yourself questions like these:

- *Am I listening to so much music that I don't have time for God or for other people?*
- *Am I using music as if it were a drug, trying to numb some pain I need to deal with?*
- *Am I so hooked on music that I can't stand the sounds of silence?*

This week, try keeping track of how much music you listen to—and what prompts you to listen. Try going without music for a day or two. You may find, as 15-year-old Jennifer says, "It's not so much that I notice it when it's playing, but I sure notice when it isn't."

If switching off the CD player gives you the shakes, you might ask yourself: *Who's in charge here, my mind or the media?*

oh, those nasty lyrics

Time spent on music can be a problem. But most battles over music aren't about hours spent, are they? They're about lyrics.

Once upon a time, one of the biggest complaints adults had against rock music was bad grammar—using "me" instead of "I" to complete a rhyme, for instance, or singing, "*Ain't* that a shame?" These days those people are stroking out just trying to make sense of the artists' *names*. ("Maybe I'll pick up this old Wu Tang Clan CD. I'm in the mood for some Chinese music.")

Twenty-first century lyrics can be hazardous to a lot more than our grammatical health. Take these lines from a recent song, for example:

@*!?* !%** @!!!*! #%! **#!??#! *@!%!!
@!!!*! #%! @*!?* !%** **#!??#! *@!%!!
#!??#! *@!%! @*!?* !% @!!!*! #%!!
#%! **#!??#! @*!?* !%** @!!!*! *@!%!!

Okay, we made that up. But if you've been listening to some of today's angrier music, you know what we're talking about.

The problem isn't just "bad words." It's the messages in some of those packages.

For instance, what are "the voices" of your favorite songs saying to you?

- That it's okay to use profanity?
- That you'd be justified in taking violent action or rebelling inwardly?
- That you're cheating yourself if you aren't sexually active?
- That suicide is an option when life isn't going your way?
- That racial slurs or comments insulting to women are acceptable?
- That it's smart to taunt or accuse God?

"Now, hold on," you might say. (There you go again.) "Even if my music has some of those messages, it doesn't matter. I just like the way it sounds. I don't listen to the words."

A lot of people say that. But I (Stan) don't. Here's why:

I learned "O Christmas Tree" in German when I was in eighth grade. I can still remember the lyrics I learned nearly four decades ago. Why? Because my eighth grade class repeated them enough times for the strange-sounding words to lodge in my brain (even though these days I can't remember where I park the car at the mall).

But that's not the whole story. Recently I heard a professional recording of "O Christmas Tree" in German, and it was so different from what I had memorized that I couldn't believe it was the same song! Our eighth-grade teacher had done his best to coach us, but that's all the German I ever learned. Of course, any time a German song is sung with a Tennessee accent, it sounds strange to begin with. But more importantly, I never compared what I had learned with actual German. When I finally did, the number of variations was rather shocking.

What Stan is trying to say with this walk down memory lane is this:

1. You may be absorbing more lyrics and other useless information than you realize.

2. If you never question what's getting lodged in your mind, you may come to believe certain "truths" that are nowhere close to God's truth.

under the influence?

If you're not convinced that lyrics are getting lodged in your brain, take this little test.

1. Can you spell the first and last names of your bologna? Most people who have heard a certain commercial jingle can.

2. Now, do you know the full names of your parents? Grandparents? Great-grandparents? Can you spell correctly the maiden names of your grandmothers? If not, does that mean they rate

lower on your priority list than your luncheon meat does?

It's not all your fault, of course. Thanks to repetition, you can get some dorky song stuck in your head to the point where a guillotine seems like the best remedy.* Repetition in music sneaks up on you. It fills your mind with things you don't necessarily care to know. Over time, it can shift your priorities, morals, and logic if you aren't careful.

"Hold it right there," you say. "Maybe I do have a few lyrics lodged in my brain somewhere. But that doesn't mean music influences what I do."

Consider a recent psychological study in an English wine shop. The store sold French and German wines. On days when the owners played French music, shoppers bought up to five times as much French wine as German. When the musical choice was German oom-pah-pah favorites, German wine outsold French.

Even some people in the music industry admit that music has influence. Take these two guys, for example:

> "If you can get their emotions going, [make them] forget their logic, you've got 'em. At MTV we don't shoot for 14-year-olds, we own them."
>
> —Bob Pittman, former MTV chairman

> "You can hypnotize people with music, and when you get them at their weakest point, you can preach into their subconscious whatever you want to say."
>
> —Jimi Hendrix, guitar legend

---

* We're kidding. Don't try this at home.

That last quote may seem a little extreme. But people have done some pretty extreme things under the alleged influence of music.

Take the case of one New Jersey 14-year-old. He got heavily involved in the occult after a research paper for school. His interest intensified as he listened to a lot of heavy metal music. Within a matter of weeks he had gone from being the friendly neighborhood paperboy to stabbing his mother to death, setting his house on fire in an attempt to kill his father and brother, and then killing himself. His dad was quoted as saying that the week before his suicide the boy had repeatedly been singing a song "about blood and killing your mother."

In California a group of boys aged 14 to 17 "formed a musical band to glorify Satan," according to a news report. They thought a human sacrifice might help them be better musicians and earn them a "ticket to hell." So they assaulted, tortured, and killed a 15-year-old girl.

Music isn't the primary problem in these instances. But it can reinforce the disturbed mental state of some young people. It has influence.

Some people use that influence to promote twisted ideas. White supremacist groups, for example, are using music to recruit kids. Mostly heavy metal, the music promotes hatred and violence toward homosexuals, Jews, African-Americans, and others. In addition to attracting young people to the groups, the hate music is sold on CDs and generates money for their perverted cause.

sound advice

It's too bad so many terrific tunes are cluttered with lyrics that don't match the quality of the music. We can appreciate it when creative artists express positive feelings in fresh, new ways. But they sometimes use coarse talk and crude images as well.

We need not blindly accept the bad lyrics with the good. Most CD players have a SKIP button, after all. If you find yourself having to push that button a lot on certain musicians' CDs, you might even decide to skip their albums completely.

This week, rather than soaking in whatever comes through your speakers or over the airwaves, why not determine what you *want* to stick in your mind and repeat *those* things? For starters, you might consider some favorite Bible verses, your parents' birthdays, or a meaningful poem.

Speaking from experience, the authors might have done better to have picked up a little more Shakespeare rather than all the verses of "Dancing Queen" and "American Pie."

they're not worthy

There's another problem we music fans sometimes run into: idol worship.

Let us explain.

We're almost confident your music isn't causing you to design golden calves for your entertainment center. But sometimes enjoying music prompts us to have too much devotion toward an artist or band.

Fan clubs and chat rooms are one thing, but some people get carried away. It's nothing new; in the late 1960s, graffiti declaring "Clapton is God" began showing up around London, glorifying guitarist Eric Clapton. The tradition carried on more recently with web pages like the one devoted to "Our Goddess —Tori Amos."

Have you ever been to a concert where you were jostling

through the crowd, fighting to get closer to the stage and the band? Imagine hearing the next day that several people had *died* from being crushed as people rushed the stage. Nine people in Denmark died that way at a Pearl Jam concert. Might your loyalty to a band (or other media celebrity) ever cause you to do things you might later regret?

Anything that gets the love, devotion, and admiration that ought to go to God alone is a potential idol. Creativity comes from God; shouldn't He get credit for it?

Here's the big test: Are you more excited about communicating with God through prayer and Bible study, or talking about your favorite musicians?

Whom do you treasure more? That's who has your heart (Matthew 6:21).

stylistic snobs

When it comes to music, we tend to like what we like, and we bond with other people who like the same stuff. That's okay. But sometimes people go a step further and ridicule those who prefer other kinds of music:

"Anybody who likes that band must be deaf."

"Only geeks like Christian music."

"He listens to metal? He must be on drugs."

With all the variety of music in the world, what gives us the right to single out one or two styles and evaluate human beings solely on whether or not they listen to the same things?

We—Stan and Randy—own around 5,000 CDs between us (and we haven't even tapped into the MP-3 bonanza yet). We listen to rock, country, pop, blues, folk, big band, a capella, soundtracks, Christian, lounge, reggae, ska, rockabilly, metal, jazz, Latin, and doo wop. You won't catch us at many operas, and we're light on classical knowledge. But we're open to all kinds of formats. We have our favorites, of course. But if we meet you and listen to what *you* like, we may be able to get to know you a little sooner and a little better.

It wouldn't be right if we rejected you because of your musical tastes. As the Apostle Paul wrote, "Do not think of yourself more highly than you ought" (Romans 12:3).

Some musical questions *are* a matter a taste, after all. That's why a Colorado judge's way of punishing people who'd violated the local noise laws—usually by playing their stereos too loudly—was so painful. Once a month he gathered the culprits and forced them to listen to songs he'd picked. Included were lounge tunes (like Wayne Newton and Dean Martin), bagpipe selections, and the *Barney* theme song. Most people sentenced to this evening of music left the courtroom determined never to break the law again and risk being subjected to such cruel and unusual punishment.

Listen to your favorite musical styles, but every once in a while turn your radio dial to a different station. See what other people enjoy. You may even begin to appreciate it—*and* them.

pump down the volume

Ever heard something like this?

"WHY DO YOU NEED TO PLAY YOUR MUSIC SO LOUD AND CAN'T YOU TURN IT DOWN BECAUSE I'M TRYING TO THINK?"

Next time someone gets on your case about the volume of your music, you might want to point out that psychologists and scientists are currently conducting studies on the sacculus, an organ in the inner ear. Fish use this organ for hearing. The theory is that when the sacculus begins to pick up sounds in excess of 90 decibels, it triggers the hypothalamus in your brain.

Loud music, it is thought, might produce the same type of thrill you would get from bungee jumping or some other sport where motion is key. According to some scientists, it might not be your imagination that music sounds better when you're at a rock concert, resting your head on the speaker, or singing loudly with a large group of friends.

If you suggest this theory to people who ask you to turn down your music, though, don't stop there. Try continuing with, "But I didn't realize I was bothering you, so I'll be glad to turn it down."

Enjoying loud music doesn't give you the right to thrust it on your parents or your neighbors. As Romans 12:10 says, "Be devoted to one another in brotherly love. Honor one another above yourselves."

Music should help bring people together, not cause divisions. Besides, loud music can damage your hearing—not to mention getting you in trouble with that judge who makes people listen to the *Barney* theme.

staying upbeat about music

So, here are some questions worth asking yourself:

Is music getting between God and me by . . .

- *taking too much of my time?*
- *stuffing my brain with messages that could eventually convince me that our relationship isn't all that important?*
- *influencing me to disobey Him?*
- *encouraging me to "worship" someone else?*
- *turning me into a snob who puts other people down?*
- *causing conflict with others who think it's too loud?*

Here are two suggestions worth trying, too:

1. *Take time for silence.*

You may feel weird when you're alone with your thoughts, but sometimes it's important to clear the clutter from your mind. A constant bombardment of music might be squeezing out a deep insight that's trying to make its way into your brain.

Besides, sometimes God speaks in "a gentle whisper" (1 Kings 19:12). Do you want to miss what He has to say?

2. *"Tithe" your listening time.*

Some people are comfortable listening only to Christian music. But if you're not one of those people, you might at least want to devote a percentage of your musical intake to songs that direct your attention to God and spiritual things. Just as we're to give God back some of the monetary blessings He's given us, you might want to offer some of your listening time in an effort to grow closer to Him.

Music is powerful. In 1997 a 21-year-old guy found that out when he got lost in the forests of Washington State. After nine days, he'd dropped 25 pounds and was dehydrated. But he started hearing flutes and bagpipes, so he followed the sound and found himself in the camp of the people who were searching for him.

As it turned out, they weren't playing any music. He had apparently hallucinated it. Somehow, even the illusion of music was enough to get him to safety.

Maybe music won't ever save your life. But if you use discernment in your musical choices, it can certainly make your life a lot richer.

"Both my parents worked, and . . . like a lot of kids growing up now, I basically had a TV there as . . . my friend and babysitter. And I do admit that I watched way too much television . . . [and] they had no idea what I was watching."
—*SHOLÉ G.*

"The more [people] see it on TV, the more they seem to be open to it."
—*ADRIAN M.*

"When you see something on TV more than once, certain people just feel they need to follow it. . . . If an artist comes out with a new style of clothing you find the next week everybody's wearing the same clothing."
—*JACQUELINE B.*

"People always talk about [how] they don't like to see the news because it makes them feel depressed, or all they see is violence on the television. And they think that's what represents the whole world. So I definitely think it affects how they feel about the world— or maybe even about themselves."
—*KIRK G.*

"Whatever it takes to get that money, you just do it. . . . If that's what people wanna hear, then they're going to give it to 'em and let 'em hear it. If that's what you wanna see, well, we'll let you see that. . . . It's all about money."
—*MARK P.*

"When some people see examples [of] black people on the news or . . . in the movies, they see us as drug dealers, gang members, we don't respect our women. So a lot of people fear us. When they see us they grab their purse. . . . It's not right because the media is not portraying what a real black woman is and what a real black man is."
—*Xica B.*

"By showing teens and kids that the next step after falling in love is going to bed with somebody, they consider that to be normal. . . . That shouldn't be acceptable."
—*Ami C.*

"If you're watching a show, what you should think is, 'Is it pure, is it noble, is it right, is it praiseworthy, is it excellent, is it admirable, is it lovely?' And [if] you think . . . 'No, it's not,' then it needs to go off. And sometimes you have to think to yourself, is it what God really wants you . . . to be watching or listening to?"
—*Chanel B.*

"So [God] says in the Scripture . . . we should put no vile things . . . before our eyes. . . . [Sometimes] when we watch TV . . . we know we're not supposed to be watching. . . . In your heart you feel that you shouldn't be watching this."
—*Marlyne J.*

"I think the guide for all of us is, take the Holy Spirit with you when you become a media consumer. . . . Ask yourself the question, 'Would I feel comfortable doing this in front of the Lord?' 'Cause that's what you're doing. As a Christian, I think you just really need to be careful."
—*Michael Warren, TV producer*

◆ ◆

a tv guide

Here are the television listings for tonight. What do you want to watch?

7 P.M.

Channel 2—*Serve-vivor.* A group of waiters compete for big tips. Each night one of them is voted out of the restaurant.

Channel 5—*Sir-vivor.* A group of Navy recruits compete in saying, "Yes, Sir!" to their captain. Each night he throws one of them off the ship.

Channel 7—*Surf-vivor.* A group of surfers see who can ride the curl the longest. Each night a loser is voted out and forced to take an office job.

8 P.M.

Channel 2—*Who Wants to Go on Medicare?* Senior citizens compete for additional medical benefits.

Channel 5—*Who Wants a Load of Underwear?* College dorm residents compete for laundry services and other big prizes.

Channel 7—*Who Wants to Shoot the Polar Bear?* Inuit

tribespeople compete for the privilege of stalking and killing a polar bear to provide for their village.

9 P.M.

Channel 2—*Wrasslin' Fever.* Cages. Piledrivers. Inattentive refs. Smackdowns. Illegal blows. Fun for the whole family.

Channel 5—*Dharma and Grace.* Tired of lawyer husbands and gay friends, two women strike up a wacky but tender friendship.

Channel 7—*Zeema, Warrior Brewer.* Sponsored by the Drink More Beer Foundation, this show is basically a bunch of actors in old-timey costumes drinking and fighting.

◆ ◆ ◆

So, what's it going to be? There are other channels, but it's more of the same.

We're joking, of course. But haven't you had nights where your actual TV viewing choices were almost as bad?

The late Elvis Presley was known for a unique method of dealing with television programs he didn't like. He would pull out a gun and blast the screen.

In this chapter we want to consider some other options. After all, you're likely to encounter some situations where you just don't have the patience for the mandatory five-day wait to get a gun license.

must-see tv?

Years ago, there were only three television channels to choose from—and sometimes a PBS station. The networks "signed off" with the "Star-Spangled Banner" at around midnight and started up again early in the morning. All you could watch at a slumber party was static.

VCRs were not yet practical household items. And network censors earned their pay; not even married couples could be shown in the same bed.

Television was a lot more "must see" back then. Most people watched one of their three options, and a common topic of conversation was "what was on last night."

TV has lost much of its allure for a lot of people, but it still has some benefits. Let's take a look at a few of them.

1. An expanded world view. Television can take you places you'll never visit in person—inside a volcano, in the deepest part of the ocean. You can actually use television to better appreciate God's creation.

TV can add to your understanding of other cultures, too. Justin, a white guy, has always lived on a large farm in a small Southern town. But TV has given him a growing sensitivity to the African-American experience, the Jewish experience, and the urban experience. TV can't fully explain the complexities of other people's lives, but it's a start.

2. Entertainment on demand. Few things in life are as convenient as television. With just the click of a button you can find pretty much whatever you're looking for, day or night. You don't have to take a shower or get dressed up, either. You can sit there in your underwear, eating Spaghettios straight from the can with a fork. Of course, you might get some strange looks from your parents' party guests, but you can do it.

3. Shared experiences. Sandi has a friend who's a big fan of the original *Star Trek.* When she comes across an episode while flipping channels, she stops long enough to watch part of it.

Later, when she tells the friend which show she saw, it makes the other person's day.

Just watching a show with family or friends helps you bond, too. And planning a party around a TV "event" like the Super Bowl can be a lot of fun.

4. *Life lessons.* Television can teach important lessons about life. Some shows are deliberately educational, but comedies and dramas can add to your understanding of relationships, self-image, and other crucial issues.

As a girl named Teresa told us, "I used to be pretty stuck up. But while watching an after-school special, I saw myself in one of the rotten characters. I decided I didn't want that reputation, so I've been trying hard to change for the better."

tv jeopardy!

In spite of TV's benefits, some people criticize it as a "vast wasteland" or the "boob tube." They warn us that we are "amusing ourselves to death." Other critics are more specific, keeping a running total of murders, other acts of violence, sexual comments, and swear words in shows.

Those are well-known drawbacks. Here are some that may be less obvious.

1. *Distorted images.* Don't try to adjust your set. The images we're talking about are the "beautiful people" and perfect hair and makeup onscreen. One of TV's unspoken messages is that tall is better than short, thin is better than fat, and a clear complexion is better than one with zits. The real world contains people with acne, frizzy hairdos, plus-size clothes—and feelings.

2. *Warped reality.* You've seen the same plot on a thousand different shows. For the first five minutes of the hour-long

drama, Jake and his dad are best friends. But then Jake wrecks the car, steals something, or otherwise incurs his father's wrath. Harsh words are exchanged, and for the next 45 minutes (including commercial breaks), Jake goes on a rage rampage. With about three minutes to go, he realizes he is at fault. He approaches his father, digs his toe into the dirt, and mumbles, "I—I'm sorry, Dad." The father gives him a big smile and a hug, and everything is okay again.

There's a reason they call this stuff fiction! In real life, it may take an angry parent (or teenager) longer than an hour to cool down. In real life, people say, "I told you so!" Friends tell you to get lost. Parents send you to your room. Teachers flunk you without changing their minds at the last minute.

3. Anything for ratings. Suppose your teachers got bonuses based on the number of homework assignments they gave you. (Perhaps you assume they do.) Might some of them slip in a few extra papers, readings, or math formulas?

TV networks get "bonuses" (higher advertising rates) based on ratings. Some programmers feel they can get a bigger bonus by showing a little more skin, bringing a character "out of the closet," or spicing up dialogue with crude language. When networks choose between more money or more morality, which do you think is going to win?

4. Falling standards. Have you noticed that some people will watch just about anything? We sit, transfixed, as one neighbor takes another to court because his goat ate some prize rosebuds. We wince (but don't stop watching) as human slabs of bacon repeatedly slam one another to the floor of the wrestling ring. We watch women with empty heads and overstuffed swimsuit tops run in slow motion down the beach.

If we stopped watching freak shows, the networks would

stop airing them. But we buy the merchandise, join the fan clubs, and rush to be first in line when the shows come to our towns. Maybe we should stop asking, "What's wrong with television?" and ask, "What's wrong with *us*?"

True, a half-hour of this stuff between chemistry and civics homework might not kill too many brain cells. But as we log hour after hour, it can erode our sensibilities as if they were an animal cracker in a vat of sulfuric acid.

5. Lack of religious understanding. A recent study showed that when faithful religious people are shown in a television program, they're portrayed positively only 11 percent of the time. When you see a minister in a comedy or drama, four out of five times he'll turn out to be evil or weird.

Why? Maybe it's because the number one rule in writing is, "Write what you know." One poll of entertainment industry decision-makers showed that a majority has "little or no faith in organized religion." If most television scriptwriters have never set foot in a church, if they know nothing about a personal relationship with God, how can they be expected to create realistic Christian characters?

Christians haven't always helped their own cause, either. A young man named Harrison remembers, "Before I knew anything about God, I would come across those Christian shows on TV and I didn't want to be any part of that. Either it would be a boring church service with someone droning on and on, or some guy would be up front, bouncing around, screaming at people, slapping them on the forehead, and watching them fall on the ground. When a friend later invited me to go to church with her, I was scared of what I would see when I got there."

6. Stereotyping. Religious people aren't the only ones

stereotyped on television. Are all old people cranky and smart-mouthed? Are all teenage boys eager to lurk outside windows and watch girls undress? Are all teenage girls ready to desert friends and family if only the right guy will pay attention to them? Do all African-American families sit around the dinner table spouting street slang to each other? You might think so if television were your only source of information.

stick or click?

So TV has its pluses and minuses. As with other forms of entertainment, you can learn to benefit from it—or you can be just another tube zombie who soaks up any bit of electronic debris that's streaming into your room.

What kinds of TV choices are you making? To find out, let's play a quick game of "Stick or Click?"

Pretend you're holding the television remote as each of the following shows comes on. Do you stick where you are at least until the next commercial? Do you pause a few seconds to see if something good is going to happen? Or do you immediately click on to the next show? Here we go!

Stick Pause Click

___ ___ ___ It's the latest music video that everyone is talking about. Many of the obscene lyrics are bleeped out, but it doesn't take a master lip reader to make out what the band is saying.

___ ___ ___ A "reality" show that you really hate—but it looks like two of the characters are getting ready to have sex.

Stick Pause Click

___ ___ ___ A comedy you personally can't stand, but all your friends love it and discuss it every week.

___ ___ ___ A big college basketball tournament.

___ ___ ___ A big professional golf tournament.

___ ___ ___ A movie based on a book you're supposed to report on next week (and haven't started to read).

___ ___ ___ A cooking show with a hip, new chef. It looks as if he might be making something with chocolate and eels.

___ ___ ___ What do you know? The Playboy Channel isn't scrambled for some reason!

___ ___ ___ *World's Worst Rabid Pet Rampages, Part 8.*

___ ___ ___ A *Simpsons* rerun. It's the one where Lisa experiences self-doubt after she is unable to work a simple puzzle.

___ ___ ___ An action/adventure movie with lots of guns, blood, and car crashes.

___ ___ ___ The Christian station is showing something from 1985 with Pat Boone.

___ ___ ___ The latest scary movie is just out on TV with the absolute worst parts edited out, but still with plenty of thrills and gore.

___ ___ ___ Some guy is ready for the $125,000 question on a quiz show.

___ ___ ___ A teen drama with your favorite actress deciding whether or not to have an abortion after getting pregnant by your favorite actor.

Stick Pause Click

___ ___ ___   It's Spring Break on one of the music stations, and the beach party crowd is really getting out of control.

Did you "stick" on any of these stations, or did you click all the way through and decide to go read a book instead? Why did you make the choices you made?

If you caught yourself pausing on imaginary stations where something "forbidden" or time-wasting was about to happen, chances are you'd do the same in real life. What kinds of choices do you think Jesus might make? Why?

Which TV choices tend to mess up your relationship with God? Which tend to keep you from spending time on things that are important to Him?

We can't answer those questions for you. You need your *own* set of guidelines to help you monitor your TV monitor.

To help you come up with those guidelines, ask yourself whether it's time to "click" in any of the following situations:

- When it's clear a graphic sex scene is coming up.
- When you've watched a half hour and nothing amusing or relevant has taken place.
- When you get to a scene that really makes you uncomfortable.
- When you need to get a big assignment done, but a great game has gone into overtime.
- When a show comes on that you've told your parents you won't watch—even if they're not home.
- When you start laughing too hard for the wrong reasons (dirty jokes, creative swear words, mockery of God, etc.).

If you don't have your own set of guidelines, you're likely to sit there like just another couch kumquat until your bladder eventually forces you to get up. Hours, days, weeks, and months of your life can be spent in suspended animation before a glowing tube if you don't create and enforce some basic rules for yourself.

We hope that before you move on to the next chapter, you'll at least give the matter some thought.

Television can offer some good learning opportunities, deep belly laughs, and relief from stress. It can also eat away your time and even your sense of right and wrong. The difference is determined by who's in control—you or the set.

There's an easy way to tell.

Next time you find yourself facing something on TV that you know you shouldn't watch, all it takes is one more click.

The only question is, are you strong enough to press the OFF button?

◆ ◆

"Actually, movies are the big influence on kids."
—BILL F.

"They compare . . . violence that takes place to things that happened in a movie. . . . People who take it heavily might go to the extreme and might be desensitized by the movies, and might go out and do something [violent] for . . . fun."
—KAI H.

"Movies that I don't allow myself to see are . . . things that I feel are degrading to women and people in general. . . . I don't want to support that kind of behavior, or that kind of thing having influence on people."
—FLORIONE W.

"To be honest . . . I pretty much watch whatever I want to. . . . I won't, like, walk out of a movie or anything like that."
—KHRISTEN B.

"I don't let myself watch R-rated movies. I try not to because the things that they show . . . [I] can find myself convincing . . . myself . . . that it is okay to go along and do those things. But it's not. . . . So I think that you can find yourself compromising with things. So that's why I've decided not to watch R-rated movies."
—SARAH S.

"I think a movie might go too far . . . but I'll still see it. I won't place any limitations on it."
—KIRK G.

"I will not allow myself to see any kind of spiritually scary movies—like movies with . . . dead ghosts coming back or whatever. I will not allow myself to see movies with a whole lot of sex in [them] 'cause I don't need that kind of stuff in my personal life. I struggle with enough things."
—*JENNIFER B.*

"We were watching a movie once together. . . . It was a movie we had rented, and we had heard [from] a few people about it. It was pretty good, and we had just . . . seen the first five minutes of it. [But] there was just so much profanity that we . . . turned it off and didn't want to watch the rest of it. . . . It was . . . bothering our spirits, so we just decided not to watch it."
—*SARAH S.*

"I think the media portrays love . . . mainly as sex and a physical act. . . . It's kind of like if you love someone, you have sex with them. . . . When it's a love story they usually end up having sex sometimes, somewhere in that movie. And I think that it kind of gives us a twisted view of what love really is."
—*JONATHAN H.*

"When you're about to go see a movie . . . you already know what's going to happen or . . . what the concept is about. So it's not a matter of [getting] 'too dirty'—you just cut it off from the starting point. Because you don't want to get to that point [when you say], 'Well, you know, I can handle this,' or . . . 'I'll turn it off then,' when you can just cut it off in the beginning. Because you don't need to fill your head and your mind . . . with that kind of stuff."
—*MARLYNE J.*

◆ ◆

"So, how'd you like those special effects?"

it came from hollywood

Hope you don't mind, but we're going to take a short break. We've written almost half the book already, and we need a breather.

Let's see if we can find a good movie on TV to watch.

Click. Kevin Bacon is making a bunch of kids walk across a rickety suspension bridge thousands of feet in the air. One of the kids looks like he's about to hurl.

Click. A guy is on his knees with his hands tied behind his back. Another guy is holding a gun to the back of his head. The guy on his knees is crying and trying to say something. Oh, man! The other guy pulled the trigger.

Click. A blond woman is standing in front of a guy's desk. Uh, now she's giving him one of those "let's get physical" looks.

Click. Two guys are walking through a cave, looking for something. One guy is holding a shotgun. I think something's coming after them, but everything's too dark to tell. Wait, here it is. It's a . . . giant rabbit. Actually, it's *not* a giant rabbit. It's obviously a regular-size rabbit that the filmmakers have tried to make *look* giant with some unbelievably bad special effects.

Aw, too bad—commercial break. "We will return to *Night of the Lepus* after these messages," the announcer says.

Click. Here's a black-and-white western. A woman is hanging out the window of a speeding stagecoach. She looks scared. The driver is either dead or unconscious. A cowboy wearing a white hat is chasing the stagecoach on his horse.

Click. A frizzy-haired, leather-wearing Olivia Newton-John is singing that John Travolta had better shape up (up, up, up) because she needs a man.

Click.

We've seen enough. We're flipping back to *Night of the Lepus.* We've got a soft spot in our hearts for really cheesy special effects and movies that are hilarious without meaning to be.

What about you?

Let's say you manage to wrestle the remote control away from us. Which movie would you flip back to? If none of the choices does much for you, there's a video store about two miles away with thousands of movies to choose from. If you want to skip the video store—and if you'll spring for the popcorn and Junior Mints—we could even stop by the local cineplex, where they've got 16 screens.

the choice is yours

But how will you choose which movie to watch? Take a look at the following factors and decide how much influence each one usually has on your movie selections.

	Big Influence	Some Influence	Little/No Influence
1. What your friends say about it			
2. How good the previews look			
3. Who's in it			

	Big Influence	**Some Influence**	**Little/No Influence**
4. Who directed it			
5. What kind of movie it is—comedy, action, horror, romance			
6. What it's rated			
7. What critics say about it			

All these factors can be helpful if you're trying to decide whether a movie is entertaining. They're usually far *less* helpful, though, if you're trying to decide whether a movie is okay to watch. Let me (Randy) give you an example.

When I was in college, I brought one of my friends home to spend Thanksgiving with my family. The first night we were there, he and I went to the video store to pick out some movies. He said we *had* to get a particular film. "It's one of the all-time classics," he said.

I trusted my friend. I knew he'd never steer me wrong.

We brought the video home and popped it in. Before long, my dad and younger sister drifted into the family room and started watching it with us. We all enjoyed the exciting story of four men who set out on an ill-fated backwoods canoe trip. Yes sir, we all enjoyed the movie—right up to the scene where one of the men is the victim of a brutal sexual attack.

For a few moments my father, my sister, and I were too stunned to move. We all just turned red and stared at each other. Finally, my father (did I mention he's a

Baptist minister?) turned to my sister and said, "I think we should go."

My friend didn't even notice them leave. He was too absorbed in his "all-time classic."

Most of the factors on the list are about as reliable as Randy's college friend. You may be able to get some useful information from them, but you can't put your trust in them. Previews (or "trailers," as they're called in the business) are good at revealing surprise endings and giving away all the funniest lines in a movie, but they can't give you the full story. Since they're usually played for general audiences, they throttle back on nudity and gore.

Previews *can* show you the *tone* of a film. If the preview seems dark and disturbing, you can bet the movie will be, too. If the preview pushes the boundaries of good taste or tries to shock you into laughing, it's safe to say you'll get more of the same in the movie.

What's more, many previews try to associate their films with other popular movies:
- "From the twisted minds that brought you [insert name of recent gross-out laughfest] comes a new comedy . . ."
- "The director of [insert name of popular gross-out horror film series] presents a new kind of terror . . ."

If you know a little about the movies mentioned in the preview, you can get a pretty good idea of what to expect in the film.

Choosing a movie based on who's in it, who made it, what it's rated, or what genre it's from isn't the answer, either. Most actors and directors have good and bad movies on their résumés. And the MPAA Ratings Board is known for making some pretty strange decisions. Some PG-13 movies have "R" written all over them, while some R-rated movies seem to have less sex and violence than most PG-rated films.

As for trusting critics, check out this statement from the lead film reviewer of a national magazine: "[The director] stages the blood-spattered violence as stylized, tongue-in-cheek spectacle, complete with chain saws and gleaming axes, that's as kicky and easy to watch as, say, the murders in the *Scream* films."

Kicky? Easy to watch? Sounds like something the whole family would enjoy!*

The most helpful feature of most movie reviews is the summary that explains the film's rating. A typical summary might say something like, "Rated R for graphic violence, drug use, sexual situations, and nudity." Those are useful details to have when you're trying to decide whether a movie is right for you or not.

Depending on others to make your movie-going decisions for you is a mistake. You can get burned faster than a treatment center for pyromaniacs. But getting information that will help you make your *own* decisions is a great idea. One website you might check out for that kind of information is *pluggedinmag.com*.

four on the cutting room floor

So, how can you decide what's okay and what's not okay when it comes to movies? If you have a relationship with God and want to please Him, are there certain films you should avoid?

Let's start with the obvious stuff. We may be going out on a limb here, but we think there are four kinds of movies we can rule out without a lot of argument.

---

* We don't mean it. We're being ironic. You knew that, right?

1. *Blasphemous movies.* These are films that make fun of God or Jesus, or portray them in unflattering or disrespectful ways. Job 37:23-24 says, "The Almighty is beyond our reach and exalted in power; in his justice and great righteousness, he does not oppress. Therefore, men revere him . . ."

Compare that with a recent film in which two fallen angels figure out a way to outsmart God (who is played by a woman) and get back into heaven. Another angel in the movie reveals that God messed up several times before finally perfecting the creation of Adam.

There are a lot of things to make fun of in this world. God isn't one of them.

2. *Occult movies.* Deuteronomy 18:10-12 offers this warning: "Let no one be found among you who sacrifices his son or daughter in the fire, who practices divination or sorcery, interprets omens, engages in witchcraft, or casts spells, or who is a medium or spiritist or who consults the dead. Anyone who does these things is detestable to the Lord . . ."

Sure, there's a difference between practicing the occult and watching movies about it. But what if a film's message is that these "detestable" things are okay or funny or exciting? Do you think God gets a chuckle out of movies like that? Neither do we.

3. *Sick movies.* These are films that cause people to shake their heads and ask, "What kind of twisted mind thinks up this stuff?" They might include movies like the one in which a psycho killer dresses up as Santa Claus and butchers families during the holiday season—and films that use cannibalism or child molestation as a source of laughs.

In Psalm 101:3, David made a promise to the Lord that we can apply to movies like these: "I will set before my eyes no vile thing."

4. *Sex movies.* We're talking about movies that are more or less compilations of sex scenes. Some critics refer to them as "soft-core porn." They're the kind of films you find on late-night pay-cable channels.

These movies, and their "hardcore" cousins, have one purpose: to spark sexual fantasies. Their message is anything but hidden: Forget God's idea that sex is only for a man and woman who are married to each other.

The Bible's "just say no" message is clear, too, in Titus 2:11-12: "For the grace of God that brings salvation has appeared to all men. It teaches us to say 'No' to ungodliness and worldly passions, and to live self-controlled, upright and godly lives in this present age . . ."

gray-area guidelines

Even after we eliminate those no-brainer categories, we're left with a wide range of movie choices—most of which still contain some sex, violence, vulgar language, or a combination of the three.

What about those? Should we give you a list of rules that would tell you where to draw the line?

Should we . . .

- set a maximum acceptable time—say, two minutes total—for onscreen sexual content? (If all the sex scenes in a movie put together total less than two minutes of screen time, would it be okay to watch?)
- give you a maximum "body count" for action or horror movies? (To meet acceptable guidelines, should a movie have fewer than five shooting deaths, four stranglings, three stabbings, or two impalings? Would one decapitation be allowed, as long as the head is not shown rolling away?)

- come up with a point system for counting and rating swear words? (Should certain words be worth one point each, others two points, and still others three? To be acceptable, should a movie have fewer than 10 total points?)

We're not going to do that. Any numbers we came up with would be either too high or too low, depending on who you ask.

What we *will* do is give you some questions to consider when you evaluate a movie:

1. *What is the tone of the movie?*

Does it excuse or even celebrate things that God is against? Are sex and violence played for laughs or cheap thrills?

2. *Is there a moral to the story?*

Are the good characters rewarded or honored? Does the film show the consequences of making wrong choices? Does it at least *suggest* that crime doesn't pay?

3. *Can anything be learned from the movie?*

Is there anything in it that will make you a wiser or better-informed person? Besides being entertained, would you gain any other benefits by watching the film?

4. *How might Jesus react to it?*

Would He laugh at the parts you laugh at? Would He cheer the same things you cheer? Would He be embarrassed? Would He recommend the film to His disciples?

5. *Might the movie worsen a problem you already have?*

If you're already developing a swearing habit, it won't help to see a film that features wall-to-wall profanity. If you're depressed, a dark, harsh story probably won't bring you up. If you have trouble with sexual fantasies, a "teen sex comedy" isn't just what the doctor ordered. To answer this question, though, you'll have to be honest about your struggles.

6. *Would you regret having scenes from this movie replay themselves later in your head?*

Like song lyrics, movie images can get lodged in your brain. That horror scene may come back to haunt you in the middle of the night. That sex scene may reappear when you're trying to resist the temptation of getting too close to a girlfriend or boyfriend. Isn't life tough enough without reruns like these?

With some movies, the answers to these questions will be obvious. With others, the answers will be harder to come by.

You may feel like a geek at first, doing "research" and answering questions about something that's "just" entertainment. But which is better: asking yourself a few questions before you buy a ticket or rent a video, or asking yourself later, "Why did I waste my time on *that*?"

let's all go to the lobby

What if, after gathering as much information as possible, you decide to see a movie—and it turns out to be a hundred times worse than you expected?

Simple: You leave. Walk out. Go for an extended visit to the snack bar. If you're with friends, tell them you'll meet them in the lobby after the show's over.

You may get a few strange looks, but that's a small price to pay if your relationship with God matters. No movie is worth more than that.

If the film is on video, the solution is even easier. Just hit the STOP button. (But be kind—please rewind.)

It takes guts to stop watching a movie in the middle. It

helps to decide in advance where your boundaries are. If a film crosses them, don't back down. Don't wait to see if things will "get better." Some theaters will refund your money if you leave early enough and explain that you're leaving because of offensive content. If yours won't, write off the money you spent on the movie as a valuable learning experience.

Before we wrap up this chapter, we should mention one other approach to movies that some people take: abstinence. These people choose not to go to *any* films—not just because of what they might see, but because they don't want to support the movie industry with their money. That may seem like the worst kind of torture, but consider this: People who abstain from movies have never had to sit through *Battlefield Earth* or anything starring Pauly Shore. (If that's not a good reason for abstinence, we don't know what is.)

Now, if there are no more questions, you'll have to excuse us. If we hurry, we should be able to catch the end of *Night of the Lepus*.

◆ ◆ ◆ ◆ ◆ ◆ ◆ ◆ ◆ ◆ ◆ ◆ ◆ ◆ ◆ ◆ ◆ ◆ ◆ ◆ ◆ ◆ ◆ ◆ ◆

"A lot of my guy friends (and a couple of the girls) at school are into these computer games. . . . They are found on MUD websites and, from what I can see, are very addicting."
—COLLEEN D.

"Personally, I don't believe that video games have as many bad effects as society really believes. However, they do put kids in front of a violent screen with them in control. They begin to learn how to be violent, and of course they are playing to win. But I know lots of good Christian guys who love video games and are still the same old boys I know. Video games may not be the best influences, but it does depend on who they're influencing."
—MISTY J.

"I think [video games] can affect kids by filling their minds with garbage. . . . Some are okay and fun. Some are completely filled with things that kids should not see. We are supposed to fill our minds with wholesome things, not things that are displeasing to God."
—ANNA J.

"Some games which are overly bloody and/or glorify the killing of other human beings can soften people into thinking that killing is okay, and those should be avoided."
—JONATHAN J.

"I do think that gory and bloody video games and movies do have an effect on people, because it makes them feel like they're powerful and it kind of makes their hearts a little hard. . . . If they do see something like a real dead body, it wouldn't really faze them."
—DANIELLE V.

"Of course there are games that are better than others. There are plenty of car racing games [and] ones with cartoon characters looking for treasure. But there are also the murderous games with guns and bombs and blood. I think the more violent games would be best avoided, but it's up to parental discretion."
—*MISTY J.*

"The biggest problem with first-person shooters is that they desensitize kids to violence, but in my case [certain] shooters ... are a great stress reliever. Unfortunately, some kids can't tell the difference between video games and reality."
—*MATTHEW W.*

"I know that [video games] can be very addictive. I have seen kids at school ... all they ever think about is video games. However, some games are intellectually stimulating, or they teach you something new. Used in moderation, I think that there are a lot of good, fun games out there to play."
—*JONATHAN J.*

"[Choosing games] depends on the maturity of the player, but certainly video games based on satanic ideas should be avoided at all costs."
—*MATTHEW W.*

"There are games that Christians should not play. It says this in the Bible—in Philippians 4:8 it talks about what you put into your head."
—*JOSH J.*

◆ ◆

"Wow! So *this* is what happens when you
beat the seventh level!"

get in the game

Here's a new video game for you to try.

It's called *Funcrushers 3000*. Your character is Norm, a teenager trying to survive in a world overrun with fun-killing zombies.

The first level is the Department Store. Your goal is to get the Golden Game from the store shelf to the door without being caught by the I.D. Watchdogs, a scary group of employees who roam the aisles and checkout counters.

Be careful—the Golden Game has an "MA" rating. That means the Watchdogs will do everything they can to keep you from leaving the store with it. Okay, choose a checkout line. But watch the cashier carefully. Look out—she's checking I.D.! Switch lines! Hurry! Whew, that was a close one.

The second level is Home Sweet Home. Your goal here is to keep the Mom and Dad characters from reading, hearing, or seeing the INR/BVG. (That's the "Important News Report about Bad Video Games." If Mom or Dad sees it, you're done.)

That's the paperboy coming up the driveway. Hurry! You've

got to get to him before he hands the newspaper to Dad. He's almost to the porch! Tackle him! Now throw the rest of his papers down the sewer drain and you won't have to worry about him for the rest of the game.

Okay, now you've got 90 seconds to find all the radios in the house and hide them in the basement. Don't forget the one hanging in the shower! Whew, you just barely made it. But you got the extra bonus minute to smash every TV in the house (except the one in your room). Just make sure no one sees you.

Look out—Mom's in the hallway! If you get caught now, you're dead. Remember to save the big screen for last. It's the hardest one to smash. Uh-oh—five seconds left. Just throw the baseball bat at the screen! Wow, you just made it!

The third level is Your Bedroom. Your goal here is to keep the Mom and Dad characters from turning off your game and dragging you away. Oh, no! You forgot to lock your door! Hurry, get out of the chair!

Aw, too late. They caught you. Drag your feet! Don't let them throw you outside! If the sunlight hits you, you're going to burn!

Too bad. Game over.

if you can't say anything nice . . .

Do any of those scenarios seem familiar?

If you're a fan of video games or computer games, you probably don't get much positive feedback about your gaming habits. Instead, you hear lots of negative comments from parents, teachers, talk show hosts, and all kinds of psychologists, sociologists, geologists (and whatever other kind of "ologists" feel the need to analyze your life). Most of the comments usually go something like this:

"Blah, blah, blah, blah, too much violence, blah, blah, blah, blah, exposing themselves to witchcraft and the occult, blah, blah, blah, blah, wasting their lives in front of a screen."

It's not that these people don't have important points to make. But none of these people seems to understand how much *fun* it is to play these games and how *cool* it is when you get good at them, right?

randy's confession

The words in this chapter may look like more "blah, blah, blah" to you. But at least we understand how and why these games become a big part of everyday life. One of us (Randy) is a member of the first generation of video gamers:

When I was nine, my dad bought us Pong, the grand-daddy of all video games. Here's how it worked. By turning a dial on the game console, you could move a paddle up and down on the screen. A white blip would bounce back and forth, and you would try to hit it with your paddle. And . . . that was it. (I know it sounds lame now, but back in the mid-seventies this was cutting-edge technology.)

Every Saturday night my dad would organize family Pong tournaments, and he and my mom and my two younger sisters and I would all take turns playing against each other. But when the weekly tournament was over, a funny thing would happen. Other family members would forget about the game and go back to their daily routine. Not me. I wanted to get better and better at the game. I wanted to be able to beat my parents without having them "pretend" to lose.

Every chance I got, I would pull the game out and practice against the computer. I practiced lining up my paddle just right and anticipating where the blip would go. Then I practiced making bank shots and reversing the direction of the blip. Then I practiced doing all those things at faster and faster speeds. In time, not only was I able to beat my parents, I was also able to beat the computer. And for a nine year old, that's a seriously cool feeling.

A few years later, my dad brought home the next development in game technology: an Atari system. This time, instead of one game to master, I had dozens. I got good at them all.

The problem was, it took so much time that my parents started to get worried—or annoyed, depending on how you look at it. They started putting restrictions on how much time I could spend playing video games. When I accused them of being unfair, they threatened to get rid of the whole system.

I couldn't imagine life without Atari, so I had to go along with their rules. One hour a day—that's what I was allowed. Looking back, it seems like a pretty good deal, but back then it felt like a prison sentence. One hour a day? One game of *Defender* could last that long!

The first couple of days were murder. That one hour every evening seemed to fly by. One night I accused my mother of setting the living room clock ahead and cheating me out of my full 60 minutes. I was losing it.

Fortunately, the madness didn't last long. After the first week or so, the thrill of playing began to wear off.

Other activities started to occupy my time. Some nights I'd play for only a half hour or so, and some nights I wouldn't play at all. Within six months, I had lost interest completely, and I never played another game of Atari.

During the rest of my high school years and into college, I spent a fair amount of time in arcades. But I never recaptured that feeling, that urgent *need* to play.

Until last Christmas. More than 20 years after I put down the Atari joystick for the last time, I bought my brother-in-law a state-of-the-art system, along with a couple of games. Christmas night, after the rest of the family had gone to bed, my sisters and I hooked up the system and started playing.

Dozens of games later, one of us finally looked at a clock and saw that it was 4:30 in the morning. So we played a few more rounds and called it a night. And for a moment—just for a moment—I got that old feeling again.

So we have an idea of what these games can mean—not just in terms of fun, but in terms of control. As a teenager, you probably don't have control over a lot of areas of your life. If your parents aren't telling you what to do, your teachers or coaches or youth leaders are. Sometimes it feels good to put yourself in charge.

And since not all of us are blessed with size, speed, and coordination, finding something we're good at can be tough. When we find a game that suits our skills, it's only natural to be excited about it.

blah, blah, blah, too much violence

How many times have people tried to tell you that the games you play are too violent? Probably more than you can count.

Dylan Klebold and Eric Harris are the ones who really put the spotlight on computer game violence. One of the first things we learned about the two guys who planned and carried out the 1999 massacre at Colorado's Columbine High School was that they were hardcore *Doom* players. Immediately "experts" started making a connection between the young men's gaming choices and their murderous actions.

Some people claimed that if the parents of Klebold and Harris had been aware of the games their sons were playing, the whole tragedy might have been prevented.

What do *you* think?

One popular response to these kinds of accusations goes something like this: "The only people who are influenced by video games are people who are already emotionally disturbed. We can't blame games for their actions. The fact that *they* went on a shooting rampage doesn't mean the games are going to affect us, too. So there's no reason for us to stop playing the games."

That's an understandable way of looking at the issue. But it's not the *only* way.

A few years ago, scientists came up with a fat substitute called Olestra. Food companies started using Olestra in things like potato chips. But the packages carried a warning: In some people, Olestra could cause diarrhea.

What would you do if someone set down a bag of Olestra chips in front of you? Would you convince yourself that only people who already have digestive problems would get diarrhea? Or would you say to yourself, "If that stuff can cause diarrhea in *anyone*, I'm going to stay away from it!"?

Fat substitutes and video games are vastly different things. But if you know that ultra-violent games have been associated with serious problems in some people, why not steer clear of those games—just to be safe? Even if the games didn't trigger the actions of Klebold and Harris, there was something about the games that appealed to their sick minds.

So what's too violent? Where do you draw the line? Are all games that involve killing bad? What about one-on-one fighting games where no one gets killed, but a lot of people get pummeled?

We're not going to draw the line for you. But we do have a suggestion that might be helpful. Invite your parents or youth group leader—whoever would be most likely to challenge and encourage you spiritually—to play (or watch you play) some of the games you're not sure about. Let them see what happens onscreen. Then ask their opinion. Use their comments to help you decide whether you should continue playing each game or not.

If you're not willing to do that, ask yourself: *Is it because I already know what they'll say, and I don't want to hear it?*

blah, blah, blah, the occult

What is it about computer and video games that brings out people's fascination with the "dark side"? Next time you're in a store that sells games, take a look at how many game boxes have pentagrams, devil's horns, or other occult symbols on them.

If you've competed online or kicked back in a gaming chat

room, you may have seen fellow gamers use nicknames like these:

DEDGOD

DKPRNC (Dark Prince)

DMNBOY (Demon Boy)

Chris, a dedicated 16-year-old gamer, offers this explanation: "It's not like we're all Satan worshipers or anything. You just want to have a nickname that's cool and a little freaky. Something, you know, that's kind of intimidating." That's why Chris calls himself SIR666 when he's online.

Is Chris right? Are the occult elements of computer games just a big put-on to make things seem more extreme and intimidating than they really are? If so, does that make it okay to play games that have occult themes?

As we mentioned in the last chapter, God doesn't exactly beat around the bush when it comes to telling us how He feels about people who mess around with witchcraft and the occult. Deuteronomy 18:10-12 says, "Let no one be found among you who sacrifices his son or daughter in the fire, who practices divination or sorcery, interprets omens, engages in witchcraft, or casts spells, or who is a medium or spiritist or who consults the dead. Anyone who does these things is detestable to the Lord."

It's hard to imagine the God who gave this warning suddenly getting lenient when it comes to computer and video games. Can you picture Him saying, "Oh, well, if you're only *pretending* to be Satan worshipers, that's different. Go ahead—have a good time"? Neither can we.

There's an old saying that goes, "When in doubt, don't." Those are probably the best words to live by when it comes to playing "dark" games. With so many games available that have nothing to do with the occult, why fool around with those that do?

blah, blah, blah, spending too much time

What's your longest gaming binge? You know the kind we're talking about. Afterward your neck aches, your fingers are stiff, your rear end is numb, and it feels like someone replaced your eyelids with sandpaper.

I (Randy) know about video game binges:

One New Year's Eve many years ago, my cousin and I played Atari from six o'clock in the evening to five o'clock the next morning. We paused only to scarf down chips and pop and yell, "Happy New Year!" to the rest of the family, which was having a party in another part of the house.

Compared to the binges of some hardcore gamers, our 11 straight hours might not be terribly extreme. But it was enough to get me thinking.

I won't deny that I had a good time for those 11 hours. But the next morning I felt I'd missed something—especially when I heard other family members talk about how much fun they'd had at the party, playing board games, telling jokes, and laughing. I began to feel regretful and a little guilty.

Maybe it had something to do with Psalm 118:24: "This is the day the Lord has made; let us rejoice and be glad in it."

Here's what it comes down to: The Lord gives us 24

hours a day to accomplish as much as we can. Spending almost half of one of those days in front of a video game screen seemed like a waste of God's gift.

Have you ever felt a deep sense of accomplishment after playing a computer game? If so, how does that compare to the feeling you might get from achieving one of the following things in the same amount of time?

- "I just learned to play a new song on guitar."
- "I just wrote a poem that explains how I feel about living in this society."
- "I just beat my best time for a two-mile run by over 20 seconds."
- "I just made a difference in a dozen kids' lives by volunteering at the children's hospital."
- "I just read a great book."

How much time should you spend on computer and video games? That's for you to figure out. If your parents set a limit, you need to honor it. If games are keeping you from more important pursuits, you need to cut back. If the controller is starting to control you . . . well, you get the idea.

virtual realities

We've been asking in this book what messages the media are trying to sell us. With video games, the message is a mindset—one that includes beliefs like these:

- The best way to vent your frustrations and anger is to blow away computer-generated characters.
- Spending a great deal of time alone in front of a screen is okay.

- Video games are the last refuge for the oppressed and misunderstood.

Think about these statements long enough, and you'll see the screwy reasoning in them.

- First, blowing away computer characters may be preferable to blowing up real people, but it's *not* the best way to deal with stress or anger. Much better ways include praying, talking with friends, and seeing a professional counselor.
- Second, spending most of your time alone, doing anything, is unhealthy. God created us with a need for human contact and interaction. When we don't get them, our mental health suffers.
- Third, even the most sophisticated games are nothing more than diversions. If you're oppressed or misunderstood, wiggling a joystick won't make a bit of difference.

There's nothing wrong with having fun in the virtual world. Just don't lose sight of your priorities and responsibilities in the real one, okay?

◆ ◆

"Although some books, magazines, and comic books should be avoided, they don't usually have the negative effects that video games do. . . . Some [kinds of reading material] are better for Christians than others. Take a look at Philippians 4:8."

—JOSH J.

"I know some books, some good devotionals . . . I have seen have very positive effects on people. But I haven't personally seen any of the opposite."

—JONATHAN J.

"If you have a whole group of kids . . . they believe in one thing and they . . . get their ideas . . . the style of clothes, what they wear, how they act—usually from TV and magazines."

—HELEN C.

"I always learned that God made us special in every single way—every different way. . . . So you shouldn't really look at somebody to be like them when you're already something. . . . I can look at magazines and get certain hairstyles, and dress certain ways, but I won't base my life just on looking like that or acting like that, talking like that, being like that. I can be my own person."

—TAMARA E.

"I'm not sure about books or comic books, but magazines have really fallen downhill. Magazines these days love to portray as much skin as possible. It gets men excited and girls get jealous. It's when the eating disorders start. Plus, many articles talk about how wonderful being gay is and other related topics. It's just not very good."

—MISTY J.

"Of course porno should be avoided because that can easily lead to other, more harmful actions. And anything ... with a lot of bad language and such in it can be harmful, and there is no point in reading it. On the flip side ... some books that deal with Christian principles can be very good for you."
—*JONATHAN J.*

"I think pornography is funny. ... Also, I think morality is relative. ... It really depends on what your definition of morality is."
—*SHOLÉ G.*

"If it was my way ... I would just take all the pornography and all the bad language and ... just scratch that right out."
—*VICTOR K.*

"Books and magazines can expose people to ideas they might not otherwise know about. Depending on what those ideas are, that could be good or bad. ... Satanic and pornographic material should be avoided. Christians should primarily read uplifting material."
—*MATTHEW W.*

"I think young people should make wise choices about what they see 'cause ... some things you can't get out of your head. No matter how hard you try to forget, you'll always remember ... what you saw. And it might come back to you, like, later on in life."
—*KAI H.*

◆ ◆

"Yeah, I read romance novels. Why?"

black and white and read all over

I (Randy) don't mean to brag, but I've lived a pretty exciting life.

When I was a kid, I had a couple of friends named Frank and Joe. The three of us used to have some unbelievable times together. The first time we hooked up we found a treasure that had been hidden in a spooky, old tower. After that it was non-stop action. In one summer alone the three of us broke up a counterfeiting ring, recovered a priceless, stolen artifact, and exposed a group of international smugglers. We even rescued a group of friends who'd been kidnapped.

As time went by, I lost contact with Frank and Joe. But the excitement in my life never stopped.

I walked all the way across America with my dog. I survived a hurricane at sea in a little fishing boat. I even played baseball with dead people—more than once.

And I never even had to leave my couch.

I lived all those adventures between the covers of books. (In case you're wondering, my old friends Frank and Joe were better known as the Hardy Boys.)

While movies can make us laugh and cry and music can change our moods, books can immerse us in another world—one that exists only in our imagination.

I've been in love with books ever since my mom read me my first Dr. Seuss.

And now I read both night and day
I read at work, I read at play
I read in buildings, I read outside
I read when I sit, I read when I ride—

Whoa, sorry. That always happens whenever I think about Dr. Seuss.

book 'em

Some kids think the only good reason to read a book is so that you don't have to fake the book report for English class. But books can transport us to exciting places. A favorite author is like a faraway friend who comes to visit every year or so and always has a great story to tell.

Book lovers have an advantage over fans of other media, too. They usually don't have to worry about people getting on their cases for reading. Books seem to be the one "legitimate" medium. You don't hear a lot of parents saying, "Why don't you put that book down and turn on the TV for a while?" Unless you're an *obsessive* reader—pasty skinned, nearsighted, and exercise deprived—you probably won't have a lot of people second-guessing your media choices.

Of course, that doesn't mean your book picks don't have to

be wise ones. You still need to ask yourself how the things you read may be affecting your relationship with God.

prose and cons

Books can introduce us to ways of thinking that we've never encountered before. They can inspire us to reexamine and appreciate our world, our relationships—even our faith.

On the other hand, you don't have to look hard to find a shelf's worth of books that aren't worth reading. Some of these feature plots, characters, scenes, and philosophies that don't meet the Bible's standard of "whatever is true . . . noble . . . right . . . pure . . . lovely . . . admirable . . . excellent . . . praiseworthy . . ." (Philippians 4:8).

Skilled writers can be extremely persuasive and entertaining. Even the worst ideas and actions, in the hands of a talented author, can be made to seem okay. Things that might convince us to turn off a TV show or walk out of a movie theater somehow don't seem as offensive in print.

Before we lose ourselves in the imaginary world of a book, we need to check the place out first and make sure it's an environment that God wouldn't mind us visiting. For instance, we can ask ourselves questions like these:

- Do the characters make an immoral lifestyle seem appealing?
- Do they learn from their mistakes or suffer the consequences of their actions?
- Do they use language that sticks in your mind—and you wish it wouldn't?

Depending on the kind of book you're considering, you'll want to ask more questions. If you're looking in the horror genre, for example, here are a few more to think about:

- Does the author seem to take pleasure in describing scenes of torture or suffering?
- Does the book tend to get you fascinated with the occult, witchcraft, demonic forces, or anything else that God warns us to stay away from?
- Are the forces of evil portrayed as being more powerful than the forces of good?

If romance is your genre, here are a few questions to consider:

- Does the book celebrate the kind of romantic love that the Bible celebrates?
- Are matters of right and wrong—like faithfulness in marriage—sacrificed in the name of "true love"?
- Would you be comfortable recommending the love scenes to your youth leader or pastor?

We could go through the entire Dewey Decimal System this way, giving you questions for each category of books, but you get the idea. No matter what kinds of books you like, it's important to keep asking questions about what you're reading.

When does a book cross the line and become "not okay"? You may be able to rely on your conscience to help you decide. Your conscience might make you uncomfortable or cause you to look over your shoulder when you read certain scenes or words. It's the inner voice that may say, "You shouldn't be reading this."

If you've learned to ignore your conscience's nagging, you may need to pray before you start a book. Ask the Lord to help you spot things that could have a negative effect on you and your relationship with Him. Ask Him to help you know when to skip a section and when to put the book down for good.

Fortunately, putting down a book isn't as awkward as walking out during a movie. You don't have to worry about explaining to your friends why you stopped in the middle. If you have a library card, you don't even have to worry about the waste of money. When you close a book and take it back to the library, all you've lost is a little time.

spineless reading material

Bookworms aren't the only ones who love reading. If you're like a lot of teenagers, you prefer to bury your nose in a comic book, graphic novel (sort of a comic books on steroids), or magazine.

Graphic novels and comic books save you the trouble of having to visualize what you're reading. Instead, they show it to you in vivid detail. Sometimes that's good (the artistry on display in many graphic novels today is astonishing), and sometimes that's not so good (the violence, sex, and occult themes on display are also pretty astonishing).

The good thing about graphic novels and comic books, though, is that you can get a pretty clear idea of what's inside just by flipping through them. Taking a minute or two at the newsstand or comic book store to thumb through the latest issue of *Masters of Infinity* will clue you in on whether it's something you should be reading. As you do, think about questions like these:

- *Is the art likely to get me fantasizing about sex?*
- *Is the tone so dark and bleak that I'll probably get depressed?*
- *Is violence used in a way that could make me less sensitive to people who suffer because of real-life violence?*
- *If I'm using this as a "crutch," trying to feel more powerful by reading about powerful characters, do I need to get real help instead?*

the 'zine scene

Whether or not you'd be caught dead with a comic book or graphic novel, you may be a magazine reader. Magazine publishers *love* teenagers, since so many kids spend so much money on the stuff magazines advertise. Publishers scramble to figure out which fashion trends, celebrities, and hot-button issues you want to read about. It must be nice to be the focus of so much attention.

If teen magazines don't do it for you, you'll probably find other periodicals that do. Enjoy putting on a fake beard and wearing plain, dark clothes? Subscribe to *Amish Impersonators Monthly.* Can't get enough of really boring playground games? Pick up this month's *Tetherball Illustrated.* (Okay, maybe these particular magazines don't exist yet, but you get the point. Whatever your interest, most likely there's a magazine for you.)

But are they really for *you*? As with other kinds of media we've covered in this book, you need to figure out what magazines are trying to sell you. It's not just cosmetics and candy bars; it's often a lifestyle and an attitude.

To help you figure out the messages in your magazines, ask yourself some questions about the articles you see listed on the cover or table of contents. Here are a few sample questions, along with actual magazine articles to which they might apply:

- Why is this article interesting to me? ("Be the Lover Your Lover Deserves.")
- Does the article try to "solve" problems I should be avoiding in the first place? ("Foolproof Hangover Remedies.")
- Does the author assume a "truth" I don't agree with? Do I need to read with an extra-skeptical eye? ("How Man Evolved: Amazing New Discoveries Reveal the Secrets of Our Past.")

- Does the article support lifestyle choices that oppose what the Bible teaches? ("How I Came Out to My Parents.")
- Does the article endorse messed-up priorities? ("Forget What Your Mother Told You: It's What's on the Outside That Counts.")
- What effect could this article have on my life if I'm not careful? ("I'm Tired of Being a Virgin.")

Most magazines are bound to run some articles you don't agree with. If it doesn't happen often, just keep reading with your "message detector" on. If an article really gets under your skin, write a letter to the editor about it. If the problems are chronic or extreme, simply cancel your subscription or refuse to buy another issue at the newsstand.

"i don't even have a pornograph to play it on!"

You didn't think we were going to talk about magazines without mentioning pornography, did you? Though statistics indicate that most people who view porn get it from the Internet, "skin" magazines are still around.

Like many guys, I (Randy) remember my first encounter with pornography:

> I was introduced to the glossy world of porn when I was about 12. A friend and I were playing basketball behind my house when we spotted a magazine sitting on top of a trash can across the alley. It's safe to say we were curious about our find. We were very interested in the magazine's hard-hitting political articles, its insightful celebrity profiles, and its humorous approach to—
>
> Okay, we wanted to look at naked women.

This magazine certainly had its share. It would be an understatement to say that my friend and I had no idea what we were looking at. We may have had vague notions of what sex was, but we certainly weren't prepared for what we saw.

Once the thrill of discovering something "forbidden" wore off, we got bored with the magazine. I can't speak for my friend, but the pictures left me feeling confused and a little grossed out. If that's what sex was, I wasn't interested.

Unfortunately, pornography leaves a lot of guys wanting more. Many experts believe it's addictive. People start out looking at so-called soft-core porn, but later find that those "tasteful" pictures aren't enough to satisfy them anymore. So they start looking for "kinkier" stuff. Their urges lead them to more and more perverted material—and, in some cases, to acting out what they've seen, committing rape or other crimes.

You may be asking yourself, *Even if there is such a thing as porn addiction, is it really that big a deal? Drugs, alcohol, and even nicotine addiction can kill you. What can porn addiction do?*

First of all, it can bring a boatload of guilt into your life—and force you to spend your time trying to hide your habit from others. How many people do you know who are proud to tell you about their skin magazine collection? When was the last time you walked into someone's house and saw *Hustler* magazine tastefully displayed on a coffee table? For most people, pornography is a vice they'd like to keep secret.

Second, pornography distorts our view of other people. It presents women (and men) as nothing more than objects. If you look at women as "things" in your fantasy life, sooner or later that attitude will carry over to your real life. It's going to make you seriously unpopular with the women around you.

Third, pornography tends to make sex a solitary experience. God wants sex to be shared between a husband and his wife. Physical intimacy was never meant to be an individual (or spectator) sport.

The apostle Paul nails the issue with his words in Romans 7:5-6:

> For when we were controlled by the sinful nature, the sinful passions aroused by the law were at work in our bodies, so that we bore fruit for death. But now, by dying to what once bound us, we have been released from the law so that we serve in the new way of the Spirit, and not in the old way of the written code.

The Lord's plan is for us to be free. As long as we're slaves to sinful habits and desires, we'll never experience the incredible things—including guilt-free sex in marriage—that God has in store for us.

If looking at pornography has become a habit for you, now's the time to put an end to it. Get rid of the porn you have now. Gather it all from the back of your closet, from under your bed, from any other places you have it hidden. Throw it away. Burn it. Rip it to shreds. Choose your own method of destruction, but get rid of it—all of it. Don't save one or two of your favorites for old times' sake. Make a clean break of it.

Next, you'll need to change the everyday patterns that contributed to your porn addiction. That may mean avoiding bookstores or other shops that carry skin magazines or videos, finding friends who aren't porn fans, and developing new interests to keep yourself busy.

You may also need to talk with a Christian counselor. A good place to start would be with your pastor or youth minister. If he's not qualified to help, he'll know of someone who is.

In their booklet "Toxic Porn" (Focus on the Family, 1999), Gene McConnell and Keith Campbell recommend the following:

> The first thing you've got to do is admit that you have a struggle with porn. . . .
>
> So, after you've admitted to yourself that you struggle, admit it to God and pray! . . . If God can raise Christ from the dead, you bet He can heal you from this problem. For some of you, there may also be issues in your past—abuse or sexual exposure, that are making pornography harder to shake. There's only so much one man can fight without help.
>
> Breaking the secrecy is absolutely, positively vital. . . . That doesn't mean everyone has to know you're struggling. Pick someone you can trust, who's listened to men's problems. A pastor, youth group leader, or counselor you can completely trust. . . .
>
> At some point, after talking the issue out with a mentor . . . [y]ou may need to spend some time with a counselor who's worked with addictions and knows what to look for and how to fix it.
>
> But taking the first step is the hardest. It really does take guts. We have this idea in our culture that a man shouldn't admit he needs help—that's pretty stupid when you think about it. What would you think of a mechanic who messed up your transmission because

he was too "macho" to tell you that you needed a specialist? If you're fighting with addiction, you need some specialists. It's not something you're supposed to be able to fix by yourself. If it were, it wouldn't be an addiction in the first place.

If you're addicted to porn, overcoming it may not be easy. But when you do, you're going to like the freedom—not to mention the way you feel about yourself.

◆ ◆

"You keep seeing things over and over again, it's going to get stuck in your head. They have a catchy jingle, it's going to work. It's all advertising."
—MICHAEL L.

"I think the thing that ads and TV are trying to do is . . . to make everybody look cool, and make things look like they're okay, like smoking. . . . They make everything like a fairy tale."
—DANIELLE V.

"[Media] affects things like body image, it affects things like the clothes you wear. You may see someone on television, a celebrity, and you're like, 'Wow, I really want that outfit.'"
—TIFFANY J.

"I think without question the media has a huge influence on society. Just look at the advertising market. Advertisers spend billions of dollars every year telling you what products to buy. And they wouldn't do that if they were convinced that that media message wouldn't change your behavior. I think that every study that I've ever seen that's done by the networks, the studios, educational organizations, tell us over and over again that we are all influenced by the media we consume."
—MICHAEL WARREN, TV PRODUCER

"A lot of times they show . . . young girls with certain looks or guys with certain looks. They feel that they have to be that certain way just to be popular or liked by different people."
—TAMARA E.

"The media doesn't make my choices for me. I make my own choices about the way I feel about everything in life. Like, you know, I want to be my own person."
—*Neil G.*

"Everybody's in it for the money—the movie producers, the record companies. . . . They like to target the youth with advertising and slogans and all that stuff . . . 'cause we're the biggest consumers and we just gobble that stuff up. We see it on TV, and hear it on the radio . . . and we want it."
—*Andrew G.*

"I think the advertisers are mainly trying to sell their products to teens and to young adults, and I think that many times they don't really care what the best interest of the person is. They just know that if you get them at a young enough age, they'll get them hooked for life and have a customer."
—*Natalie W.*

"You have to be careful with all the different ploys and all the different traps that the enemy tries to set. . . . You watch certain things or you listen to certain things and you may think it's very innocent. . . . But there's a lot of underlying things that you don't realize that . . . are going into your mind subliminally . . . things that you don't even realize that you're picking up. And I think you have to be careful of those things. . . . On TV they try to send across simple messages, and they put something else under it. . . . So you have to be careful of those little traps and little corners that you might get caught in."
—*Charles H.*

◆ ◆

"Terrible news, I'm afraid. Three teenagers in Iowa have discovered that the best things in life *are* free."

and now a word from our sponsors

Hi, I'm Randy Southern.

And this is Stan Campbell.

We hope you're enjoying *Mind over Media*. We will return you to your regularly scheduled paragraph in just a moment, but first we'd like to tell you about a few of our other publications that you might find interesting.

- *Who Wants to Beep a Millionaire: A Guide to Honking at the Wealthy* ($15.99, C & S Publications)
- *Mucus Masterpieces: A Collection of 100 Used Facial Tissues* ($24.99, Vincent Van Nose, Ltd.)
- *What Rhymes with Moo? The Year's Best Cow Poetry* ($12.99, Udder Nonsense, Inc.)

To order these and other fine products, have your credit cards ready and call 1-500-555-JUNK. Operators are standing by.

Don't reach for your wallet just yet. None of these books actually exists (though we certainly could compile a hundred messy tissues, if that sort of art appeals to you). But would it *really* surprise you to see an actual ad in the middle of this book?

Probably not. We're used to seeing ads everywhere else, so why not between chapters?

Not that all ads are bad, of course. Some TV commercials are better than the shows that sandwich them.

One of my (Randy's) favorites was an old Volkswagen commercial. A guy is doing spasmodic dance moves in his car; when his friend opens the door, you find that he's listening to "Mr. Roboto" by Styx. The commercial ends with both guys lip-synching the song while they drive.

Why did I like that so much? Probably for the same reasons you like certain commercials. It seemed to hit me just right—plus the fact that I'd lip-synched to "Mr. Roboto" at least a couple dozen times in my car when I was a teenager.

fun message, serious business

Before cable TV and satellite dishes, viewers were at the mercy of advertisers every 15 minutes or so during the broadcast day. There were usually only three or four stations to choose from, and most of them broke for commercials at the same time. You either watched the commercials or went to the bathroom. As a result, most television advertising was about as popular as head lice.

But then the balance of power shifted. Cable TV brought more channels—more places to turn to escape commercials. The ad people, desperate to keep viewers' attention, began experimenting with more eye-catching ways to get their messages across. They perfected their presentations to the point that now people are just as likely to talk about their favorite commercials as they are their favorite shows.

Marketers and advertisers have one goal in mind. Believe it or not, that goal is not necessarily to make you rush out and buy something (though no advertiser would mind if you did). What they really want from you is *brand loyalty*. Through their ads and commercials, they want to make you a *loyal* consumer of the product they're offering.

When you're looking for a new pair of shoes, they want you to look for *their* shoes. When you're looking for a bag of chips, they want you to look for *their* chips. When you're looking for commemorative Dwight and Mamie Eisenhower salt and pepper shakers, they want you to look for . . . well, you get the idea.

Creating loyalty in consumers is easier said than done. That's why advertisers pay big bucks to marketers whose job is to figure out how to influence people's buying habits. Then the advertisers pay big bucks to TV networks, radio stations, magazines, and billboard companies to run their ads. You can bet those companies wouldn't be spending that money if they didn't have proof that the ads were worth it.

target audience: you

A big chunk of that money goes toward finding out how to reach you. Well, not *just* you (so don't get cocky). As a group, though, teenagers are among the most sought-after consumers.

That's good news and bad news for you. It's good news because it's always flattering to be wanted. It's bad news because many advertisers will do almost anything to get you.

That includes targeting your weaknesses. Marketing

experts figure that most teenagers don't have the critical skills or "skeptical eye" to recognize shady sales pitches or faulty logic. They bank on the idea that you, with so much on your mind, won't stop to seriously consider the message they're sending.

They hope to dazzle and entertain you into becoming "brand loyal." They want to exploit your "gotta have it now" attitude. They want to take advantage of the pressure you feel to conform and wear the "right" clothes. And they want to do it without your even knowing it.

For each of the media we've looked at in this book, we've asked you to consider the question, "What are they trying to sell me?" With advertising, the answer is easy: everything!

Every ad has its agenda. In most cases, that agenda is to part you from your money—now and as many times as possible in the future.

But it's not always products that are being sold. Sometimes it's a lifestyle or a way of thinking. Often it's the company itself and its "attitude."

Have you ever seen a commercial in which someone actually tries to describe what Mountain Dew *tastes* like? No. All you see are the kind of people who supposedly drink Mountain Dew—radical, extreme, cool.

Have you ever heard a BMW spokesperson explain exactly why the company charges thousands of dollars more for its car than other companies charge for comparable autos? No. But you *will* hear plenty of words like *luxury, style,* and *class* thrown around.

That's all the incentive many people need. To them, buying a product is not nearly as important as associating themselves with a brand name.

ad it up

So, what can you do to keep advertising from affecting you? Should you close your eyes whenever you pass a TV, website, billboard, bus stop, logo shirt, bumper sticker, or shopping cart? Should you plug your ears whenever you're near a radio, in a store with a public address system, or on a carnival midway?

The truth is that in our culture you can't keep advertising from having some effect on you. But knowing what those effects *are* can help you lessen the impact.

First, advertising can affect your *self-image*.

Regardless of how good you feel about yourself right now, there's always room for doubt in the next five minutes. Especially when you see advertisers telling you what you *could* be if only you ...

- used this shampoo;
- wore those clothes;
- drove that car;
- splashed on this fragrance;
- followed that diet program; or
- gargled with this mouthwash.

This is where the whole being-a-teenager thing works against you. An unfortunate part of the maturing process is the struggle with insecurity about your looks, your intelligence, your social skills—everything about yourself.

Even more unfortunately, advertisers are ready to pounce on that insecurity like lions on gazelles in one of those Discovery Channel documentaries. If the fear of being publicly humiliated will cause you or your friends to buy zit cream, you can bet that some advertiser somewhere is working on a commercial in which non-zit cream users are publicly humiliated. It's nothing personal, just business.

Second, advertising can affect your *expectations*.

When most of the people on TV commercials or in magazine ads are enjoying life to the fullest with new cars, designer clothes, and nonstop partying, it's only natural to think, *Hey, why not me? I deserve that, too!*

You can start to lose perspective on what's real and what's make-believe. You can forget that more young adults work in tedious entry-level jobs than in cool dot-com companies. You may imagine that everybody watches a giant-screen TV, carries a handheld computer, and eats Big Macs and fries without gaining weight.

That leads to the third by-product of advertising. It can affect your *ability to be content*.

Instead of being thankful for the things you do have, you start to notice the things you don't have. If you let your mind dwell on the possessions you lack, your priorities begin to change. The things that once made you happy lose their ability to satisfy.

If you're a Christian, this presents special problems. Advertising can encourage us to become discontent with what God has given us—or dissatisfied with the way He made us. It can also convince us to base our value on what we have (or don't have), instead of on who we are.

You can't swing a stick in the Bible without hitting a verse that talks about being content with and thankful for all that God has given us—or one that warns us not to get wrapped up in material possessions. Here are a few:

> Do not store up for yourselves treasures on earth, where moth and rust destroy, and where thieves break in and steal. But store up for yourselves treasures in heaven,

where moth and rust do not destroy, and where thieves do not break in and steal. For where your treasure is, there your heart will be also. (Matthew 6:19-21)

What good will it be for a man if he gains the whole world, yet forfeits his soul? (Matthew 16:26)

I am not saying this because I am in need, for I have learned to be content whatever the circumstances. I know what it is to be in need, and I know what it is to have plenty. I have learned the secret of being content in any and every situation, whether well fed or hungry, whether living in plenty or in want. (Philippians 4:11-12)

see-through hype

The good news is that advertising is a lot like stage magic. Once you know the secrets behind the tricks, it's not nearly as effective. Fortunately, we don't need people like Penn & Teller or the Masked Magician to show us the secrets behind advertising. All we have to do is look at ads with a skeptical eye.

Exposing the truth behind advertising is surprisingly easy—and fun—to do. All you have to do is look for the unspoken message behind the spoken one. There's *always* an unspoken message to be found. Here are some examples.

- Hallmark Cards has used the slogan, "When you care enough to send the very best" as its spoken message. The *unspoken* message is that your friends, family members, and significant others will gauge your feelings for them by the logo on the back of a greeting card. Wouldn't it be a lot more caring to actually *make* a card yourself? Not according to our friends at Hallmark.

- Dockers came up with a simpler slogan: "Nice pants." In one commercial, a woman brought her boyfriend home to meet her family. For apparently no other reason than the fact that he was wearing Dockers, the entire family began making suggestive eye contact with the boyfriend. The commercial ended with someone (we're not sure who) rubbing a foot on his leg under the dinner table. The spoken message—or visual one, since there was no dialogue—was that if you wear Dockers, you'll draw all kinds of attention. The unspoken message was that with other pants, you couldn't draw flies if you smeared cow manure around your neck.

- In a Bud Light beer commercial, two guys took their intended purchases to a grocery checkout, only to discover that they didn't have enough money to pay for everything. They put items back one by one until they were left with only a roll of toilet paper and a six-pack of beer. When the cashier informed them that they could afford only one item, they had to make a seemingly difficult choice: toilet paper or beer. They chose the beer, then asked for a paper bag—to use as a substitute for the toilet paper. The (visually) spoken message was that Bud Light is such a special beer that it's worth sacrificing everything for it. But think: Isn't there a name for people who choose beer over food and other necessities? Oh, yeah—they're called alcoholics! An unspoken message of this commercial was that alcoholism is funny.

The more you practice spotting and rejecting unspoken messages like these, the better you'll get at making advertising work for you. Instead of seeing and hearing what advertisers want you to see and hear, you'll learn to pick out facts that are important to you. You'll be able to separate useful information—how much something costs, what kind of quality it offers, where it can be found—from meaningless hype, such as which celebrities endorse the product and what it will mean for your self-image.

you deserve a break today

At the end of the last millennium, an advertising magazine conducted a poll to choose the best TV commercials of all time. Number one on the list was an Apple ad called "1984" that introduced Macintosh computers to the world. It was filled with funky visuals of corporate drones slaving away under the watchful eye of a man on a giant video screen. The man on the screen represented IBM, which dominated the computer industry at the time. At the end of the commercial a woman carrying a track-and-field hammer smashed the video screen, symbolically freeing people from IBM's clutches.

We're asking you to do something similar when it comes to advertising.

No, don't smash your TV screen. We just want you to free yourself from the clutches of advertisers. Don't let marketers and manufacturers tell you what you need and what will satisfy you.

Exercise mind over media. Decide for yourself.

◆ ◆

"The Internet is definitely affecting our lives more and more each day.... I think it affects you only how much you let it affect you, how much you invite it into your life.... Some people choose not to use the Internet or use computers at all; other people use 'em 20 hours a day and are addicted."
—*Benjamin C.*

"I think the Internet has actually made our lives easier—although some of the things [on it] ... are completely unnecessary."
—*Sholé G.*

"Personally, I take the best things that you can get from film and television, like public television and photography on the Internet.... But there's a lot of horrible things there. ... When we grew up ... the Internet was not even existent. And nowadays kids can, you know, go to the wrong website. My little cousin who was seven came to our house and my mom walked in and he was on a gay chat room."
—*Benjamin C.*

"I think people who sit in their room, sit in their house all day and watch porn, just don't go out at all, and do nothing—it's terrible."
—*Nick S.*

"[The Internet] alienates you from actual physical contact. People think that they're communicating with more people ... but you're not actually physically dealing with people.... It's very dehumanizing, I think."
—*Benjamin C.*

"I think that . . . with the different types of media you can become desensitized real quickly . . . between movies and the Internet, between seeing violence and porn."
—DARREN F.

"[With pornography] you're basically taking images . . . on TV or the Internet and making it your life. . . . You're satisfied with just sitting there and taking in a whole bombardment of images. . . . It's not real."
—BENJAMIN C.

"They say the Internet is a world unto itself and it's an information superhighway, but I think just being out here on the sidewalk you . . . take away so much more than you would from something artificial."
—SHOLÉ G.

"I think that when King David says, 'I will set no vile thing before my eyes,' that he meant that he would keep himself away from things that might tempt him or might cause him to slip."
—JONATHAN H.

"If there's a question about 'Maybe I shouldn't be watching this,' you probably shouldn't."
—CHARLES H.

"If you know that while you're listening to something or you're watching something and inside you feel it, like, [the] Holy Spirit is . . . grieving . . . then you know that's not for you. . . . That's just like the red light."
—MARK P.

◆ ◆

"It's our new Internet filter."

10

what in the world wide web are you doing?

Suppose you visit a friend who lives in a large city you've never been to before. The friend has school during the day, but invites you to wander on your own and see the sights.

As you walk around, you come upon a number of fine restaurants with remarkably cheap food—all you can eat. The museums and libraries are roomy and have lots of exhibits that interest you. The theme parks look great and are also surprisingly affordable. The people you encounter are friendly and talkative. You start planning all the things you want to do with your friend and thinking of ways you can be invited to stay for a couple more weeks.

You walk a little further and come to a section of town that's not quite as nice. There are some off-track betting parlors, auction houses, and a number of establishments that seem quite proud to offer "Exotic Dancers."

Beyond this section of town is an even darker area. Gang

members leer at you. Kids are smoking crack in doorways. Prostitutes call out to you. Some of the sidewalks are stained with blood. Psycho killers are chasing victims with chainsaws . . .

Enough already! We've taken this analogy too far. By now you've figured out this is the chapter on the Internet, and that our city represents the electronic village you can summon at the touch of a keyboard. But don't miss our corny little point: You have the good sense to *physically* stay away from certain parts of town that are threatening and dangerous. Do you have the same good sense when it comes to the Internet?

if it's a net, you can get snagged in it

The Internet offers wonderful opportunities for education, recreation, communication, and business. No arguments there! But let's consider some of the problems that can arise.

As we write this chapter, here are some stories that have recently made the news:

- Somebody is hacking into Pentagon computers, possibly in search of military secrets.
- So many students are downloading music in our state (Illinois) that it's causing a drastic slowdown of the entire state university computer system.
- A Harvard dean has been asked to resign after pornography was discovered on his university-owned computer.
- An eighth-grader bid nearly $3 million at an Internet auction site—attempting to buy a classic convertible, a Van Gogh painting, an antique bed, a Viking ship replica, and a Superman comic. Surprisingly, he didn't actually have that much money.
- The death of more than one celebrity has been announced prematurely because of Internet postings.

• In "sting" operations, police detectives have arrested a number of people for using the Internet to meet under-age kids with the intent of having sex.

We could go on and on listing Internet problems—but frankly, we don't much care. Anytime you get a lot of people together to do *anything*, a bunch of them will do weird stuff. At most rock concerts, some fans will smoke pot. At most football games, some will get drunk. So it comes as no surprise that when the whole world connects on the same Internet system, some of them will be up to mischief—or worse.

That doesn't mean you have to join them, of course.

We can't fix everything that's wrong with the Web. What we *can* do over the next few pages is explore one question: Are *you* going places you shouldn't be going on the Internet?

depraved new world

For some people, the big Internet temptation is pornography. For others it's chat rooms, where they make themselves vul-nerable to strangers. A few get caught up in online gambling or compulsive shopping. Still others are fascinated with weird, new things—hate sites, violence, strange games.

If you're like many teenagers, you know a lot more about using computers and surfing the Web than your parents do. You may be able to check out all kinds of sites without getting caught. If your parents have installed filtering software, you may have access to friends' computers. And you know how easy it is to get to porn sites. It's all just a mouse click away.

Sometimes it happens by accident. Peter, for example, was working on a report for history class and keyed in a web address. Up popped a porn site. He later discovered the address he used was three letters off. Can you blame Peter for what happened? No—unless he goes back to the porn site on purpose.

Web page designers encourage you to "surf" the web, but surfing is not the best analogy. Many people who post web pages are *fishing*, trolling for suckers who will nibble a little bit, then a little more—and finally chomp down so hard they get completely hooked.

Educators, parents, and government leaders are on a crusade to make visual filth less accessible to young people. Pornographers are fighting back and trying to make a First Amendment free speech issue out of it. We're guessing that by the time they work something out, you'll be a grandparent.

In the meantime, what do you do when "naughty" ads or pictures pop up on your screen—and all it takes is one more click to see photos that are more graphic? Are you going to sneak a peek every chance you get, just because you can? Or do you care enough about your relationship with God to become your own filter, retreat from that site, and find something more worthwhile?

choices and consequences

The Internet presents us with a question: Should we avoid certain things only because someone is keeping us from doing them, or because we might get caught—or simply *because they are wrong?*

Let's face it. You have—or soon will have—lots of opportunities to experiment with sins of all kinds. No one will be there to stop you if you don't choose to stop yourself.

Vanessa's big brother found that out. All through high school he was an A student and active in his church youth group. His parents gave him reasonable freedom, but he always knew they were watching him pretty closely. When he went away to college, it was as if a weight had been lifted from his shoulders. No one made him study. No one stopped him from drinking. No one cared if he made it to class or not. But the university cared when he flunked out, and it revoked his full scholarship. You can be sure his parents cared when *they* found out.

The Internet provides you with similar opportunities to reject the things you've been taught. It gives you the chance to reject them in private, too. If you throw a rock through someone's window, the police could get your fingerprints and come looking for you. But on the Internet you can do things more or less in secret.

On the other hand, that also provides the opportunity for you to practice some self-discipline, to develop some Christian character.

It gives you a chance to try your hand at discernment.

The choice is yours. If you prove you can dodge Internet traps, and that you don't have to dwell on the evil you stumble across, you'll have a healthy start for making similar decisions later.

don't load this image

In chapter 8, we talked about the problem of pornography. (We were against it, in case you missed that chapter.) Is Internet porn any different? Just because you can find those images online, does that make it right? Hardly!

The things we said in chapter 8 about porn apply to the electronic version, too. (Just flip back there if you haven't read it already.) And while we're at it, here's another reason to stay away from porn sites: Once a visual image is imprinted on your mind, it's very hard to erase.

I (Stan) know that from experience:

I was at a Christian conference in Washington, D.C., where we'd all received a magazine-sized conference schedule. The people I went with were standing around in the parking garage, getting ready to go eat. As the others headed for their cars, I saw what I thought was someone's schedule on top of the pop machine. I picked it up and started to say, "Hey, someone forgot their brochure." But when I saw what I was holding, the words stuck in my throat.

It was a hard-core pornographic magazine. The image on the cover caused me to literally shudder. It was violent, sadistic, perhaps as evil as anything I've seen before or since. I immediately tossed the magazine back where I'd gotten it and left as quickly as possible.

But the image on the cover kept coming to mind repeatedly over the next few weeks. Eventually it began to fade. But like thick black paint on a white wall, it took several coats of new memories to cover it up—and I obviously still recall it from time to time.

You don't need those kinds of images messing you up. If you click into a porn site, you never know what image will be imprinted on your mind, or how long it will take to fade—if it ever does.

You've probably already had the "sex talk" at home or school. But as your curiosity grows, we hope you'll be bold enough to ask your parents or church youth leaders a lot of questions—and that you'll be honest and open about your feelings. Don't go to Internet exploiters to satisfy your curiosity, especially when people who care can help without nasty, long-range side-effects. And if you find yourself with an online pornography habit, see the advice at the end of chapter 8 on breaking free.

One other kind of website you'll want to avoid is the kind that peddles hate. You're likely to come across web pages promoting various types of my-color-is-better-than-your-color propaganda. Other sites are anti-government, anti-religion, and pretty much anti-everything-else. The best course is to back out of the site and move on to other options.

what's your screen name?

One of the Internet's dangers is that you never really know who's on the other side of the modem. The web is crawling with weirdos. Some are sick; others are sinister. You can't be sure the person at the other end of the line is really a beefy high school quarterback or a gorgeous, redheaded prom queen just because he or she says so.

Lots of people use the Internet to tell you what you want to hear, some with the hope of eventually meeting—and harming—you in person. A police precinct near us has an outstanding unit for capturing such predators—stalking the stalkers, so to speak. Officers are online around the clock, posing as teenagers and setting up meetings with people they suspect are attempting to seduce kids like you. They've arrested some pretty "respectable" people. But if they miss someone, make sure it's not the person at the other end of *your* chat line.

Don't become a victim. If you use chat rooms at all, be very deliberate about the people with whom you choose to chat. You can't know or see the other person, so admit that every contact is potentially dangerous. Stalkers are smart, and can track down victims with just a few clues—school attended, sports involvements, nicknames.

On the other hand, maybe *you* aren't always who you say you are, either.

It's tempting to use the Internet to act out your fantasies. Andrew and some of his friends like to pose as girls—just for kicks. June likes to strike up conversations with guys and pretend she's sexually experienced, when in reality she isn't.

It's all just a game. At least, that's the way it starts. But all too often the game gets out of hand.

The teenage years are turbulent enough when you try to be yourself. It's asking too much to try to be someone else. You might like to be older, taller, thinner, or richer, but playing out such fantasies on the Internet is more than playing—it's lying.

You never know what your lies may do to someone else. Maybe the person's feelings will get hurt when he or she discovers the deceit. Or maybe he or she will be encouraged to go a little further with the next person online—perhaps a person intent on more than a little "harmless" fun.

Don't try to be someone you aren't. If you find a good Internet friend, you don't want the relationship to be built on lies. Be your charming self—but more careful than usual.

where have all the hours gone?

According to one recent estimate*, if you were between the ages of 7 and 17 in the year 2000, you'll spend over *23 years* of your life online. Even if this guess is a little off, it seems clear

---

* An average from the Fortino Group, a Pittsburgh consulting firm.

that Web use will continue to soar in the future. Is that how *you* want to spend that time?

The Internet makes it awfully easy to isolate yourself for hours on end. True, it can put you in contact with knowledge and wonders and correspondents around the world. But before you lock your bedroom door forever and determine to live the rest of your life in a cyber-existence, consider two things you're giving up:

1. *The human touch.*

Let's say there's a girl named Claudia. She could e-mail you and give you one of those smiley-face emoticons. But you'd be missing the braces on her teeth, the twinkle in her eye, the freckles on her nose, and the way the wind swirls her hair around. You couldn't smell the one-of-a-kind blend of the Obsession she wears combined with the grape gum she's chewing. You couldn't hear her voice inflections or the way she giggles when you tease her.

The Internet makes one person seem pretty much like another. In spite of people's unique personalities, their fonts look the same on your e-mail. If you're not careful, you might start believing that those sending you messages are more alike than they really are. We need to keep reminding ourselves that people are individuals, not electronic clones.

In addition, psychologists will tell you of the importance of touch. It's essential for the well-being of infants, and that need continues throughout life. It means more than you might think for a friend to put a hand on your shoulder, punch you playfully in the arm, or give you a hug.

Spend too much time online, and you sacrifice many benefits of being part of the human race. It's nice to have a close friend in mind, but it's even better to have him or her within reach.

2. *The real world.*

Shopping online may save time and gas money, but in other ways it leaves something to be desired. When you walk into an actual store, the checkout girl with the blue hair and pierced nose can remind you that people are seeking recognition and identity. When the mentally challenged individual bagging your groceries smiles and speaks to you, it can remind you how fortunate you are—and how you need to share your God-given blessings with others.

Even driving to and from the store puts you in touch with the real world. Fresh air, blue skies, flowers, snow, and the neighborhood kids are among thousands of things you would miss online.

How do you suppose Jesus would deal with the Internet if He'd come today rather than 2,000 years ago? Perhaps He would e-mail a copy of the Sermon on the Mount to everyone on His mailing list. But we doubt that would ever become His main form of communication.

The Bible describes many of Jesus' actions—touching "unclean" lepers, hugging children, washing His disciples' feet, and allowing His own feet to be doused with perfume. He was always being mobbed by eager crowds; it would have been easy for Him to remain secluded. Yet He got into the thick of things, eating and partying and sailing and attending synagogue.

We shouldn't hide from the real world, either—or the people in it.

when brainwashing is good

Think about the Internet next time you're in the bathroom.

Take a look at the sink and the tub, designed to bring clean, fresh water into your home. Then look at the toilet, which is intended to rid your home of not-so-desirable stuff and carry it to the sewer system.

What if a mischievous plumber rearranged the pipes so that the clean stuff was blocked, and the raw sewage flowed *into* your home instead of out? How many of your friends would like to hang out at your place?

As gross as those prospects may seem, that's how your mind operates if you frequent the wrong sites on the Internet. Your computer works as a reverse toilet. Electronic sewage flows into your home (and your head) as long as you allow it. Don't think that won't create problems.

If it's time for a "brainwash" (in a positive sense), the best remedy is to hit the "Shut Down" command. Go outside for a while. Be around some human beings. (You might want to take a shower first.) Thrust yourself into the middle of God's creation.

Start absorbing the positive things of life. Let the world of wonder flow into your mind and replace the stench that's been accumulating.

When you're ready, the Internet will still be there. But from now on, make sure it knows who's the boss.

extra credit

If you're the residing computer expert in your household, why not ask your parents about letting you oversee Internet safety for the family? If you have little brothers and sisters—and even if you don't—consider writing a pact that family members will agree to and sign.

For example, unless your parents are around to oversee, you might want to agree not to:

• Give out photos or other personal information;

• Use a parent's credit card to order something; or

• Agree to physically meet with someone who contacts you online.

In addition, you might all agree to let other family members know when you come across something on the Web that should be avoided. You might agree never to pass yourselves off as someone you aren't. You might also agree not to go online in a room where others can't see where you're surfing.

Your own safety and peace of mind are reason enough for creating and abiding by such a pact. But if other family members are looking up to you as an example, your reasons are even better.

◆ ◆

"We spend so much time in [entertainment]. We're always in it, we're always using it. . . . Whether it's the Internet, whether it's a magazine . . . we can never really get away from it. So we're always bombarded, I guess, with pieces of media. . . . I guess we kinda pick up certain things as we go along through it."

—*JONATHAN H.*

"It's easy to walk in after a long day and just plop [in front of] the TV and veg. . . . You have to make a conscious effort, I think, to leave certain things out of your life—like watching too much television or playing on the Internet too much."

—*BENJAMIN C.*

"It's very easy to get sucked in. . . . Like [on] a rainy day— you're sitting down, you watch a good movie. And then you're like, 'Lemme see what else is on.' . . . Before you know it, it'll be 2:00. Before you know it, it's 6:00, and you just wasted your whole day watching TV. The same thing with the Internet."

—*SHOLÉ G.*

"I think you're wasting your life if you just sit on the couch all day and watch movies and TV. . . . I love music. . . . I sit in my room and listen to music, but . . . I can't do that all day."

—*NICK S.*

"I honestly wish my parents had limited my television use. They sort of [left] it up to me, and I watched a lot when I was a kid. And I definitely should have been reading more and spending more time doing other things, and I regret that."
—BENJAMIN C.

"It's easy to spend an entire day in front of a television or an entire day in front of a computer, instead of going out and experiencing the world and experiencing new things. . . . Being out in the real world you can learn so much more than you can just sitting in front of a TV or [surfing] the Internet."
—SHOLÉ G.

"Going to an art gallery, going to a concert or a sporting event, being with large groups of people and experiencing actual life . . . not on a little screen . . . is what helps me achieve [my] goals."
—BENJAMIN C.

"The Bible is a good thing to fill your mind with. . . . Choosing a career, and . . . advancing yourself in life, that's a good thing to fill your mind with. . . . You just gotta choose all the right things and not, you know, the bad things. But definitely . . . fill your mind with God."
—VICTOR K.

"Instead of spending so much time watching TV, read a book. Research some things. . . . Open up a dictionary and open up your vocabulary. . . . Spend time with yourself. Spend time with God."
—XICA B.

◆ ◆

**"It is *not* from watching too much TV.
I *always* looked like this."**

it's about time

Welcome back to *Media Challenge*—and congratulations on getting this far in our game. You are now one question away from being crowned Champion of All Media!

Here's your question:

What do the following statements have in common?

- "I don't know how people lived before TV was invented. I'd go crazy."
- "I can't stand being in the car with my mom. She either leaves the radio off or listens to Christian talk shows. It's so boring."
- "My friends and I go to movies all the time because it's the only place we can get into besides the mall—and our mall doesn't have any good stores."
- "My dad complains because I spend all my time at the computer. But he spends all his time on the golf course, so what's the difference?"

You have 15 seconds to come up with the correct answer. Go!

Da DA da da da DA da
Da DA da DA DA, da da da da da
Da DA da da da DA da
DA da da da da, da, da, boom boom.

Time's up. The answer we're looking for is *misplaced priorities*. If you got it right, you may continue to the next paragraph. If you got it wrong, please close your book now. (Okay, you can keep reading even if you got it wrong. No, really, we insist. *Please* keep reading.)

With 10 chapters down and two to go, here's where we stand. We've talked about . . .

• evaluating the music we listen to,
• monitoring our TV viewing,
• screening the movies we watch,
• deciding which video games are okay to play,
• choosing books, magazines, and other reading material,
• reducing advertising's effects on us, and
• dropping risky Internet habits.

That leaves us with one more thing to think about: getting a life.

another confession from randy

Check out the four statements at the beginning of this chapter again. Notice how they all seem to suggest that entertainment is one of life's most important things. That's what we mean by misplaced priorities.

Let me (Randy) give you an example from my own sordid past:

When I was in grade school and junior high, I would come home from school and watch reruns of *The*

Brady Bunch and *Gilligan's Island*. Day in and day out, that was my way of unwinding after class. I probably saw every episode at least five times. Some of them I knew by heart.

Now let's flash forward a few years. I graduated high school and went away to college about the time my sisters started high school. I would call home every week or so to update my parents on college life and to find out what was going on at home, but I rarely talked to my sisters or asked questions about their day-to-day lives. As a result, I kind of lost contact with them for a few years.

The point of this rather convoluted story is that to this day, I know more about the guys Marcia Brady dated in high school than the guys my sisters dated.

Okay, it's not exactly a tragic story. (In fact, I'm sure my sisters preferred that I keep my nose out of their dating lives.) But you've got to admit there's something odd and a little unsettling about knowing more about the lives of fictional characters than of family members.

If you think about it long enough, chances are you'll come up with a similar example from your own life. Let's file these stories under "Misplaced Priorities" and talk about why they happen.

One major culprit is the entertainment industry itself. Producers, programmers, and publishers go to great lengths to make us believe that their TV shows, movies, websites, books, magazines, and songs are things we can't live without. The CBS television network went so far as to use the slogan "Welcome Home" to advertise its shows, as though its stars could become susbstitute family members by appearing on our screens every week. Would watching CBS shows really be like spending meaningful time with family members?

the also-ran

At the risk of offending CBS and all other media outlets, we've got to tell you the truth. Here it is: *In the competition of meaningful ways to spend our time, the media rank no higher than a distant seventh place.*

That's right, *seventh.* No gold medal. No silver. Not even a bronze. When you get a look at the competition, you'll see why the media just can't compete.

First place goes to *our relationship with the Lord.* As we mentioned in chapter 3, Matthew 22:37-38 makes it clear: "Love the Lord your God with all your heart and with all your soul and with all your mind. This is the first and greatest commandment." Our relationship with God affects every other area of our lives. If it's not our first priority, everything else is out of whack.

The time we spend building our relationship with God includes things like Bible study, prayer, going to church and youth group, and helping with service projects. These are the activities we need to consider first when we start to fill our free time.

Second place goes to *our relationship with our family.* Your family members are the people most likely to stick with you in the future. That's one reason why it makes sense to develop good relationships with them now.

That takes time and effort, but there are millions of ways to do it:

• Find a hobby or sport that you and your father both enjoy.

- Schedule one morning a week to go to breakfast with your mom.
- Help your older brother or sister with household chores.
- Help your younger sister or brother with homework.

Better yet, come up with some ideas of your own.

We don't need to tell you stories of kids who have lost parents and siblings and wish they'd had more time with them. But the fact is that tomorrow isn't guaranteed—so it's important to carve out time for your family while you can.

Third place goes to *our relationships with our friends*. It's tempting to include the media in this category by saying, "My friends are the people I play video games with or talk to in chat rooms." But we're not talking about one-dimensional relationships here. We're talking about friendships that include all kinds of activities in all kinds of settings.

Going to movies, listening to music, and watching TV together may be part of a well-rounded friendship, but they're *just* a part. Don't forget physical things like taking hikes and riding bikes—and the emotional aspect of talking with and encouraging each other. Those things are hard to do when media images vie for your attention.

Fourth place goes to *our relationship with ourselves*. If you have a few extra hours to yourself, is your first instinct to turn on the TV, stereo, or computer? Every time you do that, you miss a golden opportunity to get to know yourself better.

The idea of spending time by yourself may seem as exciting as a paint-drying contest, but it doesn't have to be boring. Find a favorite spot where you can enjoy nature or just watch people. Think about who you are and who you want to be, what you've done and what you want to do, what you like about yourself and what you want to change. Write your thoughts in a journal or diary. You may be surprised at what you learn.

Fifth place goes to *our relationship with the rest of the world.* This would include passing acquaintances, neighbors, people at church, and total strangers—especially those who need your help. Some may go to your school; others you may know only from news reports about a famine in Africa. Some may need a cup of cold water or a listening ear; others may need to hear about your faith.

Sixth place goes to . . . *schoolwork, a part-time job, preparing for a career*—that sort of thing.

And finally . . . seventh place belongs to . . . *the media* (though it could also go to hobbies, sports, exercise, or small appliance repair).

Entertainment is fun. No doubt about that. But in terms of importance, it's really no competition for the time you spend with God and other people.

the time eater

Yet for most of us, the media occupy a big place in our lives. For some of us, entertainment is an almost round-the-clock proposition.

When was the last time you lost a couple of hours in front of a TV screen without even realizing it? Maybe you sat down to see what was on TV or to play a video game. Before you knew it, two (or three or four) hours had passed. The media beast had eaten your free time.

Unfortunately, that beast has a voracious appetite. It will gobble up any spare minute you have available.

A man named George Leigh Mallory was once asked why he wanted to climb Mount Everest. "Because it was there," he replied. That same answer often applies to our media habits.

"Why did you watch all eight hours of *The Real World* marathon?"

"Because it was there . . . on my TV."

Think of all the homework assignments and household chores you've put off until the last minute (or haven't finished at all). What percentage of those incidents had something to do with the media—a video game you were trying to master, an online chat you didn't want to leave, or a TV show you didn't want to miss? Chances are, the number is pretty high.

Maybe you don't mean for it to be that way. When you sit down, you intend to watch one show or play one game. But one game leads to two, then three. After the show you're watching ends, you flip through the channels "just to see what else is on." Before you know it, the night's gone and you're still in front of the tube.

The worst part is that often we don't even notice how much time we've lost until it's too late—until the media beast has devoured it.

the important things

Wasting a few hours here and there may not seem like a big deal. After all, you're *young*. You've got plenty of hours to spare. But each of us has only so much time to make a difference in this world. It's the kind of thing you read about in obituaries:

Mr. Ponce worked as a school counselor, volunteered at several local homeless shelters, and had seen every episode of My Mother the Car *at least five times.*

Ms. Daniels admitted that her biggest regret in life was never having reached the fourth level of Ultimate Doom.

Mr. Janikowski is survived by his mother Gladys, his father William, and his 35-inch Sony television.

Somehow these tributes don't sound right, do they?

You don't have to start writing your obituary just yet. But ask yourself whether the time you devote to the media is time you could be spending on more productive, meaningful things. We're talking about developing interests that drive you, sharpening skills that will benefit you throughout your life.

Think of people who have accomplished remarkable things in the past 50 years or so—people like Michael Jordan, Bill Gates, or your favorite musician. How much time did they spend in Internet chat rooms or in front of the TV? Probably not a lot. Those who excel in any area are the ones who devote their time and energy to studying their craft and making the necessary sacrifices to constantly improve.

How would you like to excel? What do you want to achieve? There's a world of options available:

- Learn to juggle.
- Design a website for your youth group.
- Write a poem.
- Work on your jump shot.
- Practice playing the guitar.
- Learn a second language.
- Design your own clothes.
- Paint.
- Write a song.
- Work on your golf game.
- Practice playing the piano.
- Learn to cook.
- Design a new look for your bedroom.
- Write a story.

- Work on your public speaking skills.
- Practice playing the drums.
- Draw.
- Start a running or aerobic exercise program.
- Learn to work on cars.
- "Adopt" an elderly nursing home resident.
- Research your family tree.
- Lift weights.
- Practice your photography skills.

If you want to see something amazing, choose one of these options (or come up with your own). For three months, devote your "media time" to it. If you usually watch TV two hours a day, try juggling for two hours. If you usually spend an hour and a half playing computer games, try playing the guitar for that long.

At the end of three months, you'll be astounded at the skills you've developed or the relationships you've established. You might even miss your old media friends a lot less than you thought you would.

Psalm 119:37 says, "Turn my eyes away from worthless things; preserve my life according to your word." David didn't know about today's media when he wrote that, but he did see the danger of putting too much emphasis on things that don't really matter.

Worthless things, like junk food, may be okay in small quantities. There's nothing wrong with eating a handful of chips here and there—or with being entertained occasionally.

The key is making sure that we don't overdo the junk—and spoil our appetite for what's worthwhile.

◆ ◆

"With my family and girlfriend and friends, I definitely pay attention to what they're watching, what they're listening to—the type of media they're letting into their lives and using, either to or against their benefit. . . . People who are important . . . to me . . . to know what they're putting their trust in and putting their time and energies into, it's important for me to be aware of."
—*BENJAMIN C.*

"'Don't be conformed to this world.' Don't let yourself just kinda fall into the rut and follow the crowd and do other things that other people do. But allow yourself to become . . . someone that other people can look to. . . . If they have any questions on their way to God . . . they can come to you and they can ask you."
—*JONATHAN H.*

"We should always be constantly surrounding ourselves with things that are going to bring us up—you know, Christian music, always reading our Word. Those are the excellent things. And I think those are things that we should really focus on instead of . . . the worldly music and the movies and television and things like that. Those are the things that we should keep our mind focused on, 'cause those are things that are going to eventually help us . . . in our walk with God."
—*CHARLES H.*

"I see a lot of teenagers in America today who say they're Christians, go to church, go to Christian schools, but once they leave church or Christian schools, they go out and have a totally separate lifestyle. It's like Dr. Jekyll and Mr. Hyde. And my goal is to get teenagers ... to take God, Jesus Christ, and apply Him to your life ... to be holy. I talk about music, but we could talk about a lot of issues. And our goal is for teenagers to apply Christ to their lives, to not be hypocritical, but to live the way God wants us to live so we can be testimonies and lights in this world."
—*PHIL CHALMERS, YOUTH SPEAKER*

"Be a leader and not a follower. Stand up and be what God has called you to be.... Realize that you're here for a purpose.... There's a reason why you're here. And there's not enough of us that's standing up and being and doing what we're supposed to do.... Listen.... Don't continue to let this music ... be destructive to your mind and your spirit. Be what God has called and created you to be."
—*L.G. WISE, RAP ARTIST*

"When you listen to God, you're not being gypped. You're getting greater than what you want to get.... He gives you more than what you want."
—*MARLYNE J.*

"That choice is ours. He's a God who doesn't want ... to make us love Him. He's a God that wants us to love Him on our own. So He cares what we see and ... listen to. But as a people, it's up to us to make that change."
—*XICA B.*

◆ ◆ ◆ ◆ ◆ ◆ ◆ ◆ ◆ ◆ ◆ ◆ ◆ ◆ ◆ ◆ ◆ ◆ ◆ ◆

"Mom...Dad...I'd like to talk to you about how your media choices may be negatively impacting my social life."

12

a little help for your friends

Well, here you are at the final chapter of this book. If you've read straight through (and didn't just jump to the end to see how it turns out), we're glad you did. We hope you are, too.

We also hope you know more about your media choices than you did when you started. But what about the choices *other* people in your life are making when it comes to entertainment? Are they affecting you? Are you affecting them?

hey, hey, what would you say?

Here's a little quiz. How would you respond to each of these people?

1. Tiffany loves romantic movies where the guy and girl argue throughout, but wind up in love (and usually in bed). Personally, you don't think the sex scenes are appropriate and tell her so. She replies, "I like these movies. You like your kind of movies. I don't criticize what you watch, so why do you feel the need to get on my case?"

2. Kimberly is a Christian who comes to you with a problem:

159

"My parents keep telling me I should listen only to Christian musicians, but most of them are pretty lame compared to the ones I like. Why should I listen to inferior music just because the lyrics are 'Christian'?"

3. Jasper challenges you: "If you're a Christian, you're supposed to be stronger than Satan and all that devil stuff, right? So why are you so afraid to go online and play some of my favorite games with me just because they have a few flaming skulls here and there?"

4. Karl says, "Okay, I admit my favorite bands swear a lot and have some violent lyrics. But in the liner notes a lot of them say, 'Thank you, God,' or 'Thank you, Jesus.' Aren't they using their talent for God, just like Christian artists do?"

Each of these kids is giving you a chance to be a positive influence. Will you take it? Let's look at some responses you might make.

1. Tiffany has raised the "my opinion versus your opinion" argument. It's pretty intimidating; you probably don't want to come off sounding judgmental by saying your stuff is okay and someone else's isn't.

One way to avoid that problem is to elevate the argument above the movie (or song or website or TV show). For example, you might explain that what really bothers you is what the film *does* to you. You might say something like, "I'm not comfortable going to those movies with you because they make me start fantasizing about sex, and that's something I try not to do."

Tiffany should understand that, since hormones rage through most teenagers at a rate that makes Niagara Falls seem like a slow drip. You're not putting her down; you're just explaining how those movies affect you (and may affect her).

2. If you agree with Kimberly that Christian alternatives to music, movies, video games, and other forms of entertainment aren't always up to the same production standards as the "secular" ones, say so. Either way, you have an opportunity to find common ground. You could pull out some of your favorite songs from Christian artists (if you have some) and see what she thinks. Or the two of you can begin a joint search for better Christian media—and there *is* some good stuff out there.

3. Jasper might not understand that as a Christian, you want to keep dark and violent thoughts from cluttering your mind (Philippians 4:8). You also want to avoid getting interested in things that God has declared off limits (Deuteronomy 18:10-12). In addition, Jasper needs to know that while God is certainly greater than Satan, the devil can easily whip *your* bony posterior if you drift away from the Lord. You could explain that weeding out certain influences is a way of expressing your loyalty to Jesus.

4. Karl may not realize how easy it is to declare yourself a Christian and not act like one. You might explain that in order for God's people to honor Him, they need to practice what they preach. No one is perfect, of course, but those who are committed to God will keep trying to "clean up their act" throughout their lives.

In cases like these, base your responses on your understanding of what the Bible says. And be honest. It's okay to say, "It's a struggle for me to stay away from sexual and violent things," or "Sometimes I feel like I'm missing out on a lot of stuff everyone else seems to be doing." It's also good to explain, "But I try to do what pleases God, and I think that makes for a better life."

You and a friend can argue all day about whether or not a movie has "too much skin" or a song has "too many swear words." But when you identify the real issues (like rebelling against authority, shrugging at premarital sex, isolating yourself from other people, or simply eating up too much time), you have something to reason about. Then your opinion takes on more weight, and may even influence someone else.

is opportunity knocking, or is that your knees?

If you know what your non-Christian friends are watching and listening to, you may have good opportunities to talk to them about God.

When the Apostle Paul was traveling and telling people about Jesus, he went through the city of Athens. There he saw an altar dedicated "to an unknown God." Paul used this chance to tell the people, "Now what you worship as something unknown I am going to proclaim to you" (Acts 17:23). He then told them about the *real* God, and how Jesus had risen from the dead.

As a result, some laughed at him. But several others became believers.

If you watch and listen closely, you'll find many references to "unknown gods" in the media. Lots of people are searching for spiritual truth, and are recording their progress in songs, films, books, and websites.

Some have reached some mistaken conclusions along the way. They may believe an acceptable response to life's pressures is taking drugs, because they haven't discovered the comfort of God's love. Others may follow a god of violence because they don't know God's peace. Still others are intrigued by the mystique of Eastern or New Age beliefs because they think Christianity has been tried and failed.

Songs and movies reflecting these opinions can create great opportunities for spiritual discussions. For example, a few years ago a popular song asked the question, "What if God was one of us?" When her friends sang or mentioned that song, Jackie liked to tell them that God *was* one of us when Jesus was on earth—and is still among us.

This doesn't mean you have to spend hours soaking up media in order to have something to talk about with spiritual seekers. Nor does it mean you should watch and listen to junk, calling it "research." Keep using that *Discernment* button.

You don't have to "convert" someone with every conversation, either. Just stay alert to opportunities God might send your way. You may be surprised at how many times you'll be able to have a positive influence.

a final word of warning

On the other hand, there's another possibility. Have you ever considered that your media choices might influence your friends *negatively?*

Perhaps you're able to appreciate shows and songs in which the artists express doubt that God exists. Instead of shattering your faith, the honest expression of doubt challenges you and prepares you for when the topic comes up in real life. Or you're able to read a book that expresses suicidal feelings—without feeling that way yourself. You keep reading because you want to understand and help someone else.

But not everybody is that way.

Not everyone is good at tuning out potentially damaging

messages. Chances are that many of your friends can't watch or listen without being influenced.

Just as you wouldn't offer a drink to a recovering alcoholic, you don't want to be listening to bleak and hopeless music around someone who has suicidal tendencies. You don't want to loan a lunatic friend a copy of *Bomb Making for Dummies*, either.

Media can be what the Bible calls a "stumbling block" for others. In the early church days, a big issue was whether or not it was okay to eat meat that had been offered to idols. The Apostle Paul was spiritually strong. He knew that idols were nothing but rocks and wood. If he could get some prime steak at a good price, he probably wouldn't think twice about whether it had sat in front of an idol. But others who weren't as strong in their faith might see what he was doing and fear he was pledging loyalty to gods other than Jesus. So to prevent being a "stumbling block" to such people, Paul was willing to quit eating meat altogether (1 Corinthians 8:9-13).

Even if you think you can maneuver around all of today's media hazards, there is perhaps no bigger stumbling block for many of your friends. Be careful that one of your entertainment choices doesn't cause problems for "anyone with a weak conscience." If it does, you might need to shelve it for the good of the other person. You're going to be an influence one way or another, so make sure you're a *positive* one.

so long, farewell, *auf wiedersehen,* goodnight
Throughout most of this book, we've tried to answer the question, "What difference does it make what I watch and listen to?" In this chapter we've tried to address the query,

"What difference am I making in my world because of the opportunities provided by the media?"

If you have good answers to either one, we'd love to hear your stories. We'd also be happy to hear your questions and comments about your experience in the Media Jungle. You can write to Focus on the Family at one of the following addresses:

Focus on the Family
Colorado Springs, CO 80995

Focus on the Family
P.O. Box 9800
Stn. Terminal
Vancouver, B.C. V6B 4G3

◆ ◆ ◆

So, when it comes right down to it, why should you exercise mind over media?

Consider this: "No eye has seen, no ear has heard, no mind has conceived what God has prepared for those who love him" (1 Corinthians 2:9).

The media will continue to present your eyes, ears, and mind with some amazing sights, sounds, and experiences. But loving God and investing in your relationship with Him offers far more. No matter how much you see and hear, if you put God first, you ain't seen nothing yet!

about the authors

Stan Campbell earned degrees in recording industry management at Middle Tennessee State University and in communications at Wheaton Graduate School. He's been involved in youth ministry for 25 years and has written more than 30 books, most recently *The Complete Idiot's Guide to the Bible* (Alpha Books).

Randy Southern, who earned a degree in mass communications at Taylor University, has spoken to youth groups on the subject of media discernment. A former youth product developer, he works as a freelance writer and editor. His books include *It Came from the Media* (Victor) and *What Would Jesus Do* (Youth Specialties).

Awesome Resources

MIND OVER MEDIA: THE POWER OF MAKING SOUND ENTERTAINMENT CHOICES

You can't escape the ideas and images that come from the media—nor should you have to! So how do you weed through the bad and grasp the good? In this video, unlike any other, Lakita Garth hosts a fast-paced, hard-hitting selection of discussions with students, prisoners, music stars and youth culture experts who probe the media. You'll be challenged to evaluate what you see and hear in simple, yet powerful ways.

LIFE ON THE EDGE—LIVE!

Tune in! Dial up! Speak out!

This award-winning, national radio call-in show hosted by popular youth speakers and authors Joe White and Susie Shellenberger gives teens like you something positive to tune in to every Saturday night from 9 p.m. to 10 p.m. Eastern time. You'll get a chance to talk about the hottest issues of your generation—in fact, no topic is off limits! So check it out and be challenged to think out loud and offer hope to others. See if it airs in your area by visiting us on the Web at www.lifeontheedgelive.com.

MY TRUTH, YOUR TRUTH, WHOSE TRUTH?

Who's to say what's right and wrong? Isn't taking a stand arrogant, judgmental and intolerant? Author Randy Petersen shatters the myth that everything is relative and shows teens that absolute truth does exist. It matters and is found only in Christ! Paperback. Understand more about this critical topic in the unique video *My Truth, Your Truth, Whose Truth?*

NO APOLOGIES: THE TRUTH ABOUT LIFE, LOVE AND SEX

Read the truth about sex—the side of the story Hollywood doesn't want you to hear—in this incredible paperback featuring teens who've made decisions about premarital sex. You'll learn you're worth the wait—and understand the painful realities of sex before marriage. Discover more benefits of abstinence in the video *No Apologies: The Truth About Life, Love and Sex*

MASQUERADE

In this hard-hitting 30-minute video, popular youth speaker Milton Creagh uses unrehearsed footage of hurting teens to "blow the cover" off any illusions that even casual drug use is OK.

to *Fire Up Your Faith!*

FROM THE DARE 2 DIG DEEPER SERIES:

FANTASY WORLD

The perfect images that society portrays to teen girls are far from reality. Find out how to keep a godly perspective and have thoughts grounded in reality.

IN YOUR FACE . . . IN YOUR MIND

Pornographic images are everywhere today. Most are targeted to teen guys. Find out how to resist falling to this addictive sin.

LYRICS DON'T MATTER?

With a lighthearted style, one man shares his personal journey from being obsessed with secular music to choosing Christian music. This fun-to-read booklet reminds readers to use their power of discernment.

GETTIN' REAL: TV VS. REALITY

In this eye-opening booklet, you'll take a straightforward look at the "unreal" lifestyles of television characters and what happens behind the scenes to develop them.

GREAT FICTION READING STARTS HERE!

THE CHRISTY MILLER SERIES

Teens across the country adore Christy Miller! She has a passion for life, but goes through a ton of heart-wrenching circumstances. Though the series takes you to a fictional world, it gives you plenty of food for thought on how to handle tough issues as they come up in your own life! Includes books 10, 11 and 12.

THE NIKKI SHERIDAN SERIES

An adventurous spirit leads Nikki Sheridan, an attractive high school junior, into events and situations that will sweep you into her world and leave you begging for the next book in this captivating six-book set!

ARE YOU READY TO LIVE LIFE ON THE EDGE?

At Focus on the Family, we are committed to helping you learn more about Jesus Christ and preparing you to change your world for Him! We realize the struggles you face are different from your mom's or your little brother's, so Focus on the Family has developed a ton of stuff specifically for you! They'll get you ready to boldly live out your faith no matter what situation you find yourself in.

We don't want to tell you what to do. We want to encourage and equip you to be all God has called you to be in every aspect of life! That may involve strengthening your relationship with God, solidifying your values and perhaps making some serious changes in your heart and mind.

We'd like to come alongside you as you consider God's role in your life, discover His plan for you in the lives of others and how you can impact your generation to change the world.

We have Web sites, magazines, palm-sized topical booklets, fiction books, a live call-in radioshow . . . all dealing with the topics and issues that you deal with and care about. For a more detailed listing of what we have available for you, visit our Web site at www.family.org. Then click on "Resources," followed by either "Teen Girls" or "Teen Guys."

TRYING TO REACH US?

In the United States:
Focus on the Family
Colorado Springs, CO 80995

Call 1-800-A-FAMILY
(1-800-232-6459)

In Canada:
Focus on the Family
PO Box 9800
Stn. Terminal
Vancouver B.C. V6B 4G3

Call 1-800-661-9800

To find out if there is an associate office in your country, visit our Web site:
www.family.org

WE'D LOVE TO HEAR FROM YOU!